More Praise for *Remote*

"What you'll find in *Remote* is profound advice from guys who've succeeded in the virtual workforce arena. This is a manifesto for discarding stifling location- and time-based organizational habits in favor of best work practices for our brave new virtual and global world. **If your organization entrusts you with the responsibility to get things done, this is a must-read."**

—David Allen, internationally bestselling author of
Getting Things Done: The Art of Stress-Free Productivity

"Remote is the way I work and live. Now I know why. If you work in an office, you need to read this remarkable book, and change your life."

—Richard Florida, author of the national bestseller *The Rise of the Creative Class: And How It's Transforming Work, Leisure, Community and Everyday Life*

"In the near future, everyone will work remotely, including those sitting across from you. You'll need this farsighted book to prepare for this inversion."

—Kevin Kelly, senior maverick for *Wired* magazine and
author of *What Technology Wants*

"Leave your office at the office. Lose the soul-sapping commutes. Jettison the workplace veal chambers and banish cookie-cutter corporate culture. **Smart, convincing, and prescriptive, *Remote* offers a radically more productive and satisfying office-less future, better for all (well, except commercial landlords)."**

—Adam L. Penenberg, author of *Viral Loop: From Facebook to Twitter, How Today's Smartest Businesses Grow Themselves*

"Shows how remote working sets people free—free from drudgery and free to unleash unprecedented creativity and productivity. The first gift copy I buy will be for my boss!"

—James McQuivey, PhD, VP and principal analyst at Forrester Research, and author of *Digital Disruption: Unleashing the Next Wave of Innovation*

"Just like we couldn't imagine a cell phone smaller than a toaster in the 1970s, some companies still believe that they can't get great performance from their employees unless they show up at an office. **Virtual work is the wave of the future, and Jason and David do a brilliant job of teaching best practices for both employees and employers.**"

—Pamela Slim, author of *Escape from Cubicle Nation: From Corporate Prisoner to Thriving Entrepreneur*

"Jason and David convincingly argue the merits of remote work, both from the perspective of manager and of worker . . . **Remote work gives you the power to craft your own life, and this book is a road map to get that.**"

—Penelope Trunk, author of *Brazen Careerist: The New Rules for Success*

"The decentralization of the workplace is no longer fodder for futurists, it's an everyday reality. *Remote* **is an insight-packed playbook for thriving in the coming decade and beyond.**"

—Todd Henry, author of *The Accidental Creative: How to Be Brilliant at a Moment's Notice*

"*Remote* **shows you how to remove the final barrier to doing the work you were meant to do, with the people you were meant to do it with, in the most rewarding and profitable way possible—this book is your ticket to real freedom!**"

—John Jantsch, author of *Duct Tape Marketing: The World's Most Practical Small Business Marketing Guide*

"*Remote* **is not just a powerful toolbox . . . It's full of fascinating insights into collaboration, innovation, and the human mind.**"

—Leo Babauta, author of *Zen Habits: Handbook for Life*

AUTHORS' NOTE

When we started writing this book in 2013, the practice of working remotely—or telecommuting, as it's often referred to—had been silently on the rise for years. (From 2005 to 2011 remote work soared 73 percent in the United States—to 3 million workers total.[*])

The silence was loudly broken at the end of February 2013, though, when Yahoo! announced that they were dismantling their remote-work program, just as we were finishing this book. All of a sudden, remote work moved from academic obscurity to a heated global conversation. Hundreds, if not thousands, of news articles were written, and controversy was in the air.

Of course, we would have appreciated Yahoo!'s CEO Marissa Mayer waiting another six months for our pub-

---

[*] http://www.globalworkplaceanalytics.com/telecommuting
-statistics

lication date. That said, her move provided a unique backdrop against which to test all of *Remote*'s arguments. As it turned out, every single excuse you'll find in the essay titled "Dealing with excuses" got airtime during the Yahoo! firestorm.

Needless to say, we don't think Yahoo! made the right choice, but we thank them for the spotlight they've shined on remote work. It's our aim in this book to look at the phenomenon in a much more considered way. Beyond the sound bites, beyond all the grandstanding, what we've provided here is an in-the-trenches analysis of the pros and cons—a guide to the brave new world of remote work. Enjoy!

INTRODUCTION

The future is already here—it's just not
evenly distributed.

—WILLIAM GIBSON

Millions of workers and thousands of companies have already discovered the joys and benefits of working remotely. In companies of all sizes, representing virtually every industry, remote work has seen steady growth year after year. Yet unlike, say, the rush to embrace the fax machine, adoption of remote work has not been nearly as universal or commonsensical as many would have thought.

The technology is here; it's never been easier to communicate and collaborate with people anywhere, any time. But that still leaves a fundamental people problem. The missing upgrade is for the human mind.

This book aims to provide that upgrade. We'll illuminate the many benefits of remote work, including access to the best talent, freedom from soul-crushing commutes, and increased productivity outside the traditional office. And we'll tackle all the excuses floating around—for example, that innovation only happens face-to-face, that people can't be trusted to be productive at home, that company culture would wither away.

Above all, this book will teach you how to become an expert in remote work. It will provide an overview of the tools and techniques that will help you get the most out of it, as well as the pitfalls and constraints that can bring you down. (Nothing is without trade-offs.)

Our discussion will be practical, because our knowledge comes from actually practicing remote work—not just theorizing about it. Over the past decade, we've grown a successful software company, 37signals, from the seeds of remote work. We got started with one partner in Copenhagen and the other in Chicago. Since then we've expanded to thirty-six people spread out all over the globe, serving millions of users in just about every country in the world.

We'll draw on this rich experience to show how remote work has opened the door to a new era of freedom and luxury. A brave new world beyond the industrial-age belief in The Office. A world where we leave behind the dusty old notion of outsourcing as a way to increase work output at the lowest cost and replace it with a new ideal—one in which remote work increases both quality of work and job satisfaction.

"Office not required" isn't just the future—it's the *present*. Now is your chance to catch up.

THE TIME IS RIGHT
FOR REMOTE WORK

Why work doesn't happen at work

If you ask people where they go when they really need to get work done, very few will respond "the office." If they do say the office, they'll include a qualifier such as "super early in the morning before anyone gets in" or "I stay late at night after everyone's left" or "I sneak in on the weekend."

What they're trying to tell you is that they can't get work done at work. The office during the day has become the last place people want to be when they really want to get work done.

That's because offices have become interruption factories. A busy office is like a food processor—it chops your day into tiny bits. Fifteen minutes here, ten minutes there, twenty here, five there. Each segment is filled with a conference call, a meeting, another meeting, or some other institutionalized unnecessary interruption.

It's incredibly hard to get meaningful work done when your workday has been shredded into work moments.

Meaningful work, creative work, thoughtful work, important work—this type of effort takes stretches of uninterrupted time to get into the zone. But in the modern office such long stretches just can't be found. Instead, it's just one interruption after another.

The ability to be alone with your thoughts is, in fact, one of the key advantages of working remotely. When you work on your own, far away from the buzzing swarm at headquarters, you can settle into your own productive zone. You can actually get work done—the same work that you couldn't get done at work!

Yes, working outside the office has its own set of challenges. And interruptions can come from different places, multiple angles. If you're at home, maybe it's the TV. If you're at the local coffee shop, maybe it's someone talking loudly a few tables away. But here's the thing: those interruptions are things you can control. They're passive. They don't handcuff you. You can find a space that fits your work style. You can toss on some headphones and not be worried about a coworker loitering by your desk and tapping you on the shoulder. Neither do you have to be worried about being called into yet another unnecessary meeting. Your place, your zone, is yours alone.

Don't believe us? Ask around. Or ask yourself: Where do you go when you *really* have to get work done? Your answer won't be "the office in the afternoon."

Stop commuting your life away

Let's face it: nobody likes commuting. The alarm rings earlier, you arrive home that much later. You lose time, patience, possibly even your will to eat anything other than convenience food with plastic utensils. Maybe you skip the gym, miss your child's bedtime, feel too tired for a meaningful conversation with your significant other. The list goes on.

Even your weekends get truncated by that wretched commute. All those chores you don't have the will to complete after slugging it out with the highway collect into one mean list due on Saturday. By the time you've taken out the trash, picked up the dry cleaning, gone to the hardware store, and paid your bills, half the weekend is gone.

And the commute itself? Even the nicest car won't make driving in traffic enjoyable, and forget feeling fresh after a trip on most urban trains and buses. Breathe in the smell of exhaust and body odor, breathe out your health and sanity.

Smart people in white coats have extensively studied commuting—this supposedly necessary part of our days—and the verdict is in: long commutes make you fat, stressed, and miserable. Even short commutes stab at your happiness.

According to the research,* commuting is associated with an increased risk of obesity, insomnia, stress, neck and back pain, high blood pressure, and other stress-related ills such as heart attacks and depression, and even divorce.

But let's say we ignore the overwhelming evidence that commuting doesn't do a body good. Pretend it isn't bad for the environment either. Let's just do the math. Say you spend thirty minutes driving in rush hour every morning and another fifteen getting to your car and into the office. That's 1.5 hours a day, 7.5 hours per week, or somewhere between 300 and 400 hours per year, give or take holidays and vacation. Four hundred hours is exactly the amount of programmer time we spent building Basecamp, our most popular product. Imagine what you could do with 400 extra hours a year. Commuting isn't just bad for you, your relationships, and the environment—it's bad for business. And it doesn't have to be that way.

---

* "Your Commute Is Killing You," *Slate,* http://www.slate.com/articles/business/moneybox/2011/05/your_commute_is_killing_you.html

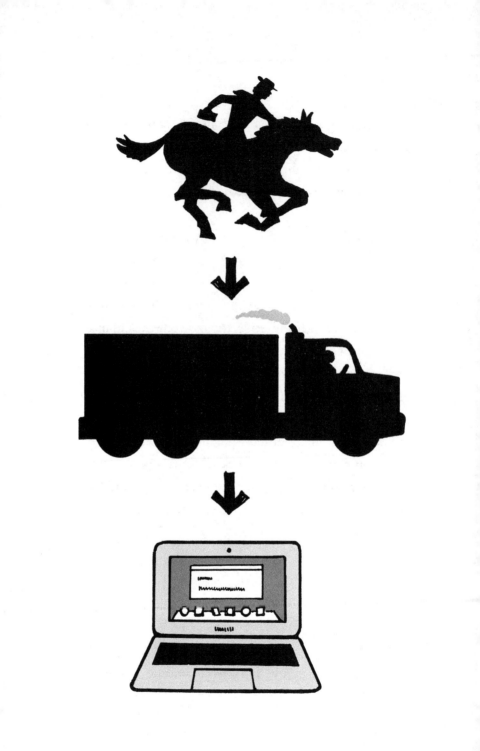

It's the technology, stupid

If working remotely is such a great idea, why haven't progressive companies been practicing it all along? It's simple: they couldn't. The technology just wasn't there. Good luck trying to collaborate with people in different cities, let alone halfway around the world, using a fax machine and FedEx.

Technology snuck up on us and made working remotely an obvious possibility. In particular, the Internet happened. Screen sharing using WebEx, coordinating to-do lists using Basecamp, real-time chatting using instant messages, downloading the latest files using Dropbox—these activities all flow from innovations pioneered in the last fifteen years. No wonder we're still learning what's possible.

But past generations have been bred on the idea that good work happens from 9am to 5pm, in offices and cubicles in tall buildings around the city. It's no wonder that most who are employed inside that model haven't considered other options, or resist the idea that it could be any different. But it can.

The future, quite literally, belongs to those who get it. Do you think today's teenagers, raised on Facebook and texting, will be sentimental about the old days of all-hands-on-deck, Monday morning meetings? Ha!

The great thing about technology, and even working remotely, is that it's all up to you. It's not rocket science, and learning the tools that make it possible won't take that long either. But it *will* take willpower to let go of nostalgia and get on board. Can you do that?

Escaping 9am–5pm

The big transition with a distributed workforce is going from synchronous to asynchronous collaboration. Not only do we not have to be in the same spot to work together, we also don't have to work at the same time to work together.

This is one of those things that's born out of necessity when collaborating with people in multiple time zones, but it benefits *everyone*, even those in the same city. Once you've structured your work technique and expectations to deal with someone seven hours ahead in Copenhagen, the rest of the home office in Chicago might as well work from 11am to 7pm or 7am to 3pm—it's all the same.

The beauty of relaxing workday hours is that the policy accommodates everyone—from the early birds to the night owls to the family folks with kids who need to be picked up in the middle of the day. At 37signals, we try to keep a roughly forty-hour workweek, but how our employees distribute those hours across the clock and days just isn't important.

A company that is efficiently built around remote work doesn't even have to have a set schedule. This is especially important when it comes to creative work. If you can't get into the zone, there's rarely much that can force you into it. When face time isn't a requirement, the best strategy is often to take some time away and get back to work when your brain is firing on all cylinders.

At the IT Collective, a film production and video marketing firm based in Colorado (but with people in New York and Sydney too), the team of editors will occasionally switch to nocturnal mode when working on a new film. It's simply how they get their best work done. The next day the editors will overlap with the rest of the team just long enough to review progress and get direction for the next night. Who cares if they slept way past noon to make that schedule work?

Naturally, not all work can be done entirely free of schedule restrictions. At 37signals, we offer customer support to people on American business hours, so it's important our customer support team is available during that time. But even within those constraints, relaxed schedules are still a possibility so long as the group as a whole is covering the full spectrum.

Release yourself from the 9am-to-5pm mentality. It might take a bit of time and practice to get the hang of working asynchronously with your team, but soon you'll see that it's the work—not the clock—that matters.

End of city monopoly

The city is the original talent hub. Traditionally, those who ran the engines of capitalism thought: "Let's gather a large number of people in a small geographical area where they must live on top of each other in tight quarters, and we'll be able to find plenty of able bodies to man our factories." Most splendid, Sir Moneybags!

Thankfully, the population-density benefits that suited factories proved great for lots of other things too. We got libraries, stadiums, theaters, restaurants, and all the other wonders of modern culture and civilization. But we also got cubicles, tiny apartments, and sardine boxes to take us from here to there. We traded the freedom and splendor of country land and fresh air for convenience and excitement.

Lucky for us, the advances in technology that made remote working possible have also made remote culture and living much more desirable. Imagine describing to a city dweller of the 1960s a world in which everyone has access to every movie ever made, every book ever written, every album ever recorded, and nearly every sports game live (in higher quality and better colors than at any time in the past). Surely, they would have laughed. Hell, even in the 1980s they would have laughed. But here we are living in that world.

There's a difference, though, between taking it for granted and taking it to the logical conclusion. If we now have unlimited access to culture and entertainment from any location, why are we still willing to live bound by the original deal? Is that overpriced apartment, the motorized sardine box, and your cubicle really worth it still? Increasingly, we believe that for many people the answer will be no.

So here's a prediction: The luxury privilege of the next twenty years will be to leave the city. Not as its leashed servant in a suburb, but to wherever one wants.

The new luxury

A swanky corner office on the top floor of a tall building, a plush company-provided Lexus, a secretary. It's easy to laugh at old-money corporate luxuries. But the new-money, hip ones aren't all that different: a fancy chef and free meals, laundry services, massages, a roomful of arcade games. They're two sides of the same coin.

That's the coin given in exchange for the endless hours spent at the office. Away from your family, your friends, and your extracurricular passions. The hope is that these enticements will tide you over during those long years when you're dreaming of all the things you'll do when you retire.

But why wait? If what you really love doing is skiing, why wait until your hips are too old to take a hard fall and *then* move to Colorado? If you love surfing, why are you still trapped in a concrete jungle and not living near the beach? If all the family members you're close to live in a small town in Oregon, why are you still stuck on the other coast?

The new luxury is to shed the shackles of deferred living—to pursue your passions *now*, while you're still working. What's the point in wasting time daydreaming about how great it'll be when you finally quit?

Your life no longer needs to be divided into arbitrary

phases of work and retirement. You can blend the two for fun and profit—design a better lifestyle that makes work enjoyable because it's not the *only* thing on the menu. Shed the resentment of golden handcuffs that keep you from living how you really want to live.

That's a much more realistic goal than buying lottery tickets, either the literal or figurative ones. As an example of the latter: pursuing a career-ladder or stock-option scheme and hoping your number hits before it's too late to matter.

You don't need to be extraordinarily lucky or hard-working to make your work life fit with your passions—*if* you're free to pick where to work from and when to work.

This doesn't mean you have to pick up and move to Colorado tomorrow, just because you like skiing. Some people do that, but there are many possible in-betweens as well. Could you go there for three weeks? Just like working from the office, it doesn't have to be all or nothing.

The new luxury is the luxury of freedom and time. Once you've had a taste of that life, no corner office or fancy chef will be able to drag you back.

Talent isn't bound by the hubs

If you talk to technologists from Silicon Valley, moviemakers from Hollywood, or advertising execs from New York, they'll all insist that the magic only happens on their sacred turf. But that's what you'd expect talent hub nationalists to say. You're the fool if you believe it.

"Look at the history," they'll say, pointing to proud traditions bearing glorious results. Yes, yes, but as the fine print reads on investment materials: "Past performance is no guarantee of future results."

So here's another set of unremarkable predictions: The world's share of great technology from Silicon Valley will decline, the best movies of the next twenty years will consist of fewer Hollywood blockbusters, and fewer people will be induced to buy products from admen in New York.

Great talent is everywhere, and not everyone wants to move to San Francisco (or New York or Hollywood, or wherever you're headquartered). 37signals is a successful software company started in—gasp!—the Midwest, and we're proud to have hired spectacular employees from such places as Caldwell, Idaho, and Fenwick, Ontario.

In fact, we don't have a single employee in San Francisco, the hub where every technology company seems to be tripping over itself to find "rock stars" and "software ninjas." This hasn't been a conscious choice on our part, but given the poaching games being played in major hubs, with people changing jobs as often as they might reorder their iPhone playlists, it's not exactly a net negative.

When you have dozens, even hundreds, of competitors within walking distance of your office, it should come as no surprise when your employees cross the street and join the next hot thing.

As we've observed, star employees who work away from the echo chambers of industry spend far less time brooding about how much greener the grass is on the other side and, generally, seem happier in their work.

It's not about the money

When people hear the term "remote workers," they often think "outsourcing." They assume that remote work is just another ploy dreamed up by business fat cats to cut costs and ship jobs to Bangalore. That's an understandable gut reaction. It's also wrong.

Letting people work remotely is about promoting quality of life, about getting access to the best people wherever they are, and all the other benefits we'll enumerate. That it may also end up reducing costs spent on offices and result in fewer-but-more-productive workers is the gravy, not the turkey.

Though our suggesting that remote work benefits *both* employer and employee may sound overly chipper and have you thinking of the sentiment expressed in those cheesy posters from the 1990s, WIN-WIN!, the reality is that, for everyone, there *is* much to like about the practice. Too much writing on work is pitched as either pro-employer or pro-worker. While those struggles are real, they're not the struggles we're interested in examining.

Besides, the key intellectual pursuits that are the primary fit for remote working—writing, programming, designing, advising, and customer support, to mention just a few—have little to do with the cutthroat margin wars of, say, manufacturing. Squeezing slightly more words per hour out of a copywriter is not going to make anyone rich. Writing the best ad just very well might.

But saving is always nice

So remote work isn't primarily about the money—but who doesn't like saving as a side effect? It certainly makes a great argument if you're trying to convince a manager.

Money, in fact, is the perfect Trojan horse for getting the bean counters on your side. Make them see dollar signs where you see greater freedom, more time with the family, and no commute, and you'll both get what you want.

When trying to convince said bean counters, there's no logic like big company logic—so here's some from IBM,[*] the bluest of blue chips:

> Through its telework strategy, since 1995, IBM has reduced office space by a total of 78 million square feet. Of that, 58 million square feet was sold at a gain of $1.9B. And sublease income for leased space not needed exceeded $1B. In the U.S., continuing annual savings amounts to $100M, and at least that much in Europe. With 386,000 employees, 40 percent of whom telework, the ratio of office space to employee is now 8:1 with some facilities as high as 15:1.

---

[*] "Working Outside the Box," IBM white paper, 2009

Who can argue against billions saved? Certainly not the gang trying to get you to save on staplers and printing paper. And the savings aren't just for the company. While the firm's owners get to save on office space, the employee gets to save on gas. HP's Telework Calculator* shows a savings of almost $10,000 per year for an SUV driver who spends an hour a day commuting ten miles round trip.

Cutting back on commuting also means huge savings for the environment. That same IBM study showed how remote work saved the company five million gallons of fuel in 2007, preventing more than 450,000 tons of CO_2 emissions to the atmosphere in the United States alone.

Helping the company's bottom line, adding to your pocketbook, and saving the planet: check, check, check.

---

* http://www.govloop.com/telework-calculator

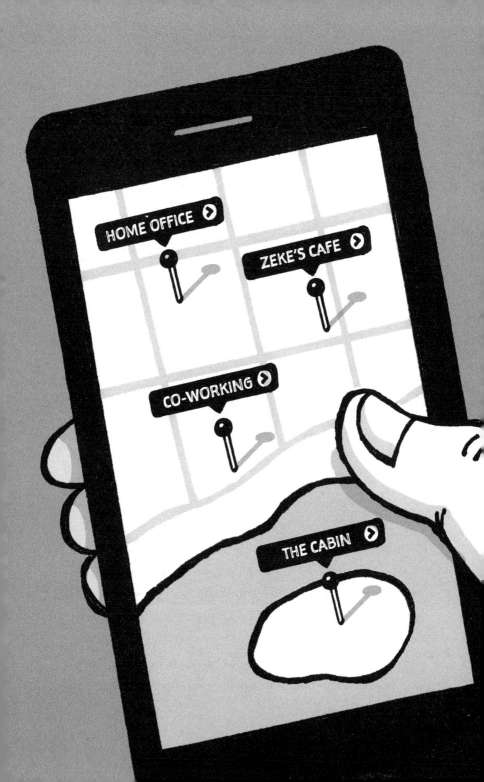

Not all or nothing

Embracing remote work doesn't mean you *can't* have an office, just that it's not required. It doesn't mean that all your employees *can't* live in the same city, just that they don't have to. Remote work is about setting your team free to be the best it can be, wherever that might be. Across companies, large and small, flexible remote-working strategies can be found in all sizes and shapes. Furniture maker Herman Miller's knowledge and design team is entirely remote, working from ten different cities around the United States. At digital communications company Jellyvision 10 percent of the workforce is completely remote, another 20 percent works from home a couple days a week, and the rest work regularly from the company headquarters in Chicago.

In 1999, 37signals' original team of four began with a nice, traditional office in Chicago. After a few years, we realized it didn't make sense for us—the place was too big, the rent too high—so we got rid of it. We moved to the corner of another design firm, where we rented a handful of desks for $1,000 per month. Soon we had more than a handful of employees, but it didn't matter. David joined from Copenhagen, and over the years we hired more programmers and designers from all over the world. But we stayed in that design-firm corner, saving rent and enjoying the hassle-free setup, for close to a decade!

Now we have thirty-six employees and a West Loop Chicago office we helped design. It's got a small theater for presentations and a ping-pong table, and on any given day ten employees work there. Is it worth it? We think so, but we wouldn't have said the same thing ten years ago, and probably not even five. Is it required? Absolutely not, but we've earned it. It's a luxury, not a necessity—although it sure is nice that a few times a year all our employees can fly in for a company-wide gathering, and we have an awesome space to meet.

For other companies where the trappings of success are an important part of the image—for example, advertising agencies or law firms or C-level recruiting outfits—having a showy office may make sense. Acknowledging that the office is there to impress clients sets an owner or manager free to make it the best theater experience it can be—and employees can remain free to work from home when they're not needed as extras for the scene.

Still a trade-off

It's easy to feel euphoric about the wonders of working remotely. *Freedom, time, money—we get it all. There'll be honey in my backyard and milk on tap.* But calm down, Winnie. Remote work is not without cost or compromise. In this world very few leaps of progress arrive exclusively as benefits. Maybe the invention of the sandwich, but that's it. Everything else is a trade-off, and you'll be wise to know what you're getting into.

At first, giving up seeing your coworkers in person every day might come as a relief (if you're an introvert), but eventually you're likely to feel a loss. Even with the substitutes we'll discuss, there are times when nothing beats talking to your manager in person or sitting in a room with your colleagues, brainstorming the next big thing.

The same goes for the loss of imposed structure and regimen. It requires a new level of personal commitment to come up with—and stick with—an alternative work frame. That's more responsibility than may be apparent at first, especially for natural procrastinators—and who isn't from time to time?

And what about the family men and women who choose to work from home? It's not always easy to set boundaries. Kids will be kids, demanding your attention *right now*, and your spouse, just like a coworker, might not realize that an interruption to show you the Internet's latest hit meme is not what the productivity doctor ordered.

The key is not to think of any of this as exclusively good or bad. Rather, you should just focus on reaping the great benefits and mitigating the drawbacks. We'll show you how.

You're probably already doing it

Your company may already be working remotely without your even knowing it. Unless it has its own lawyers on staff, it likely outsources legal work to an independent lawyer or a law firm. Unless your company has its own accounting department, it likely outsources accounting to a CPA. Unless your company has its own HR systems, it likely outsources payroll, retirement, and health care to outside firms. And what about all those companies that hire ad agencies to help communicate their message to the market?

Legal, accounting, payroll, advertising—all essential business activities. Without outside people to perform these key functions you might not even *be* in business. All these activities are carried out outside your company's walls, away from your company's network, and outside of your management's direct control—and yet there's no doubt it's all being done efficiently.

Every day this kind of remote work works, and no one considers it risky, reckless, or irresponsible. So why do so many of these same companies that trust "outsiders" to do their critical work have such a hard time trusting "insiders" to work from home? Why do companies have no problem working with a lawyer who works in the next town over and yet distrust their own employees to work anywhere other than their own desks? It just doesn't make sense.

Worth counting too is the number of days you spend at the office emailing someone who sits only three desks away. People go to the office all the time and act as though they're working remotely: emailing, instant messaging, secluding themselves to get work done. At the end of the day, was it really worth coming to the office for it?

Look around inside your company and notice what work already happens on the outside, or with minimal face-to-face interaction. You may be surprised to discover that your company is more remote than you think.

DEALING WITH EXCUSES

Magic only happens when we're all in a room

You know the feeling. Everyone's sitting around a table, ideas are building on ideas, and intellectual sparks are lighting up the room. It's tempting to think that this kind of magic only happens when people can see and touch each other.

Let's assume for a second that's true: Breakthrough ideas only happen when people meet face-to-face. Still, the question remains: How many breakthrough ideas can a company actually digest? Far fewer than you imagine. Most work is *not* coming up with The Next Big Thing. Rather, it's making better the thing you already thought of six months—or six years—ago. It's the work of work.

Given that, you're only going to frustrate yourself and everyone else if you summon the brain trust too frequently for those Kodak moments. Because either it means giving up on the last great idea (the one that still requires follow-up) or it means further stuffing the backlog of great ideas. A stuffed backlog is a stale backlog.

This is why at 37signals we don't meet in person all that often. Our attitude is, we need a clean plate before going up for seconds. Only about three times a year does the whole company get together in the Chicago office. And even that can be a tad too frequent if our goal is to really blow it out on the free-riff idea ramp!

But what about those spur-of-the-moment rays of brilliance?! First, few such rays actually warrant the label "brilliant"—more likely they're mere rays of enthusiasm (and not to be confused with a priority). Second, you'd be amazed how much quality collective thought can be captured using two simple tools: a voice connection and a shared screen. Every time we use something like WebEx, we're surprised at how effective it is. No, it's not 100 percent as effective—it lacks that last 1 or 2 percent of high-fidelity interaction—but it's much closer than you'd think.

By rationing in-person meetings, their stature is elevated to that of a rare treat. They become something to be savored, something special. Dine out every once in a while on those feasts and sustain yourself in the interim on the conversation "snacks" that technology makes possible. That will give you all the magic you can handle.

If I can't see them, how do I know they're working?

Most fears that have to do with people working remotely stem from a lack of trust. A manager thinks, *Will people work hard if I'm not watching them all the time? If I can't see them sitting pretty at their desks, are they just going to goof off and play video games or surf the web all day?*

We'll let you in on a secret: If people really want to play video games or surf the web all day, they're perfectly capable of doing so from their desks at the office. In fact, lots of studies have shown that many people do exactly that. For example, at clothing retailer J.C. Penney's headquarters, 4,800 workers spend 30 percent of the company's Internet bandwidth watching YouTube videos.[*] So, coming into the office just means that people have to put on pants. There's no guarantee of productivity.

People have an amazing ability to live down to low expectations. If you run your ship with the conviction that everyone's a slacker, your employees will put all their ingenuity into proving you right. If you view those who

---

[*] "J.C. Penney Exec Admits Its Employees Harbored Enormous YouTube Addiction," http://www.huffingtonpost.com/2013/02/25/jc-penney-employees-youtube_n_2759028.html

work under you as capable adults who will push themselves to excel even when you're not breathing down their necks, they'll delight you in return.

As Chris Hoffman from the IT Collective explains: "If we're struggling with trust issues, it means we made a poor hiring decision. If a team member isn't producing good results or can't manage their own schedule and workload, we aren't going to continue to work with that person. It's as simple as that. We employ team members who are skilled professionals, capable of managing their own schedules and making a valuable contribution to the organization. We have no desire to be babysitters during the day."

That's just it—if you can't let your employees work from home out of fear they'll slack off without your supervision, you're a babysitter, not a manager. Remote work is very likely the least of your problems.

Unfortunately, not everyone takes such a sensible approach. The poor employees of Accurate Biometrics have to endure constant remote surveillance by their boss, who uses InterGuard[*] software to monitor their computer screens. Apparently that's a growing trend. InterGuard alone claims ten thousand clients, and research

---

[*] "'Working From Home' Without Slacking Off," *Wall Street Journal,* July 11, 2012

group Gartner estimates that 60 percent of employees will suffer from some sort of Big Brother invasion by 2015. Yikes!

The bottom line is that you shouldn't hire people you don't trust, or work for bosses who don't trust you. If you're not trusted to work remotely, why are you trusted to do anything at all? If you're held in such low regard, why are you able to talk to customers, write copy for an ad, design the next product, assess insurance claims, or do tax returns?

As Sir Richard Branson commented in his ode to working remotely: "To successfully work with other people, you have to trust each other. A big part of this is trusting people to get their work done wherever they are, without supervision."*

Either learn to trust the people you're working with or find some other people to work with.

---

* "Give people the freedom of where to work," http://www.virgin .com/richard-branson/give-people-the-freedom-of-where-to-work

People's homes are full of distractions

Between soap operas, PlayStation, cold beers in the fridge, and all the laundry that needs doing, how can you possibly get anything done at home? Simple: because you've got a job to do and you're a responsible adult.

Okay, we're all human and we all occasionally fall prey to temptation. We may as well admit that, yes, the home may contain more distractions and temptations than the average office cubicle. But having recognized the problem, we can work to do something about it. Keep in mind, the number one counter to distractions is interesting, fulfilling work. While flipping burgers is unlikely to keep anyone intellectually stimulated for long, most modern remote-friendly jobs are certainly capable of doing so.

Sometimes, distractions can actually serve a purpose. Like the proverbial canary in the coal mine, they warn us—when we feel ourselves regularly succumbing to them—that our work is not well defined, or our tasks are menial, or the whole project we're engaged in is fundamentally pointless. Instead of reaching for the video game controller or turning on soap operas, is it perhaps time to raise your voice and state the obvious? If you're feeling like this, chances are others are too.

Of course, sometimes it's not the worthiness of the work task that's the issue—rather, it's that we've set ourselves up for failure. If you're working on the couch in front of the TV, well, it's tempting to reach for the remote. If you're sitting in the kitchen, you may find yourself thinking of emptying the dishwasher. But if you're sitting in a dedicated room intended for work with the door closed, you stand a far better chance of staying on task.

If that's not possible, or not enough, you can always try working outside the house entirely. Just because you're working remotely doesn't mean that it always has to be from your house. You can work from a coffee shop or the library or even the park.

But in reality goofing off is much less of an issue than people fear. It's like taking a nice vacation. It's great to be away from work for a couple of weeks, but there's only so much time you can spend lying on a beach blanket or exploring Paris before that gets boring too.

Most people *want* to work, as long as it's stimulating and fulfilling. And if you're stuck in a dead-end job that has no prospects of being either, then you don't just need a remote position—you need a new job.

Only the office can be secure

Companies often go to great lengths to make employees run software on the company's own servers rather than over the Internet, only to let executives carry around unencrypted laptops. It's no good having the tallest castle walls if you leave the drawbridge down.

Security is a big and serious deal, but it's also largely a solved problem. That's why the average person is quite willing to do their banking online and why nobody is afraid of entering their credit card number on Amazon. At 37signals, we've devised a simple security checklist all employees must follow:

1. All computers must use hard drive encryption, like the built-in FileVault feature in Apple's OS X operating system. This ensures that a lost laptop is merely an inconvenience and an insurance claim, not a company-wide emergency and a scramble to change passwords and worry about what documents might be leaked.

2. Disable automatic login, require a password when waking from sleep, and set the computer to automatically lock after ten inactive minutes.

3. Turn on encryption for all sites you visit, especially critical services like Gmail. These days

all sites use something called HTTPS or SSL. Look for the little lock icon in front of the Internet address. (We forced all 37signals products onto SSL a few years back to help with this.)

4. Make sure all smartphones and tablets use lock codes and can be wiped remotely. On the iPhone, you can do this through the "Find iPhone" application. This rule is easily forgotten as we tend to think of these tools as something for the home, but inevitably you'll check your work email or log into Basecamp using your tablet. A smartphone or tablet needs to be treated with as much respect as your laptop.

5. Use a unique, generated, long-form password for each site you visit, kept by password-managing software, such as 1Password.* We're sorry to say, "secretmonkey" is not going to fool anyone. And even if you manage to remember UM6vDjwidQE9C28Z, it's no good if it's used on every site and one of them is hacked. (It happens all the time!)

6. Turn on two-factor authentication when using Gmail, so you can't log in without having ac-

---

* https://agilebits.com/onepassword

cess to your cell phone for a login code (this means that someone who gets hold of your login and password also needs to get hold of your phone to login). And keep in mind: if your email security fails, all other online services will fail too, since an intruder can use the "password reset" from any other site to have a new password sent to the email account they now have access to.

Creating security protocols and algorithms is the computer equivalent of rocket science, but taking advantage of them isn't. Take the time to learn the basics and they'll cease being scary voodoo that you can't trust. These days, security for your devices is just simple good sense, like putting on your seat belt.

WHO WILL answer THE PHONE?

Who will answer the phone?

When clients or customers call or email during their normal business hours, they'll surely expect a timely response, regardless of where your workforce is located or the hours you keep. You simply have to deal with that.

But that doesn't mean you can't set some expectations. Jellyvision, for example, asks their Fortune 500 customers not to schedule meetings with them before 10am to better fit remote workers in different time zones.

If you occasionally have to commit an hour or two to a call at odd hours, it's not exactly the end of the world. Being available for a one-off 11pm or 5am must-do phone call is a small price to pay for the freedom of remote work.

At 37signals, we make sure that our customer support department is always staffed during Chicago business hours, plus as much on either side as we can cover. That doesn't mean everyone has to work the 9am–5pm Central Time shift, though. If you have some people working 6am–2pm, some working 8am–4pm, and others working 11am–7pm, you can cover the whole day and more, and never miss an email or a call.

Of course, this might not be as easy if you're a tiny company with just one or two people responsible for dealing with clients. In that case, yes, you may well have to assign "regular working hours" to those employees whose chief function is to answer customers. But why subject everyone in the company to those hours? False equality benefits nobody.

Working remotely isn't without complication or occasional sacrifice. It's about making things better for more people more of the time.

Big business doesn't do it, so why should we?

Many big businesses get away with staggering amounts of inefficiency and bureaucracy and seem fine for years. Once a corporate behemoth has built a big fat moat around a herd of cash cows, who cares how many cow herders they have or how little they get done?

That's a roundabout way of saying that looking to big business for the latest productivity tips is probably not the smartest thing to do. The whole point of innovation and disruption is doing things differently from those who came before you. Unless you do that, you won't stand a chance.

So it really doesn't matter that Multinational, Inc., forbids its employees to work from home. In fact, you should be happy if the 800-pound gorilla in your industry is still clinging to the old ways of working. It will just make it that much easier to beat them.

The same is true if you actually do work at a big business. Big businesses love to look at what each other is doing too. But if you hide in the herd, you're not likely to get ahead of the pack.

All you need is confidence—confidence that you see a smarter way of working even when everyone else in your industry is sticking to business as usual. That's how great ideas evolve from being fringe crazy to common knowledge. Taking advantage of working remotely is one of those ideas. It'll be common knowledge and practice soon enough, but why wait?

Breaking routine is never without struggle, of course. Fighting the established wisdom of the day is never a free ride. Fortunately, some big companies already get it. Just to mention a few who've fully embraced working remotely: IBM, S.C. Johnson & Son, Accenture, and eBay. Are those big enough for you?

Others would get jealous

If you're pitching your boss to let you work from home a few days a week, a common rebuff is how envious your coworkers would be if you were granted this special privilege. *Why, it simply wouldn't be fair! We all need to be equally, miserably unproductive at the office and suffer in unity!*

First of all, if working remotely is such an obvious good thing that everyone would want it, why *shouldn't* we let everyone do it? Is the business we're talking about just an elaborate scheme to keep everyone in their assigned seats for a set number of hours? Or is it rather an organization of people getting work done? If it's the latter, why not let people work the way they prefer, and judge everyone on what—not where—work is completed?

Second, of course it's true that some jobs simply aren't a good fit for remote execution. If a vital function is to send packages to customers and that requires access to inventory, well, that task is not going to happen from home. But so what? Why force everyone in the organization to work the same way? The guy sending packages from the warehouse already has a different job from the girl running the books in accounting. Different jobs, different requirements. People get that.

The best way to defuse the "everyone must be bound

by the same policy" line of argument is to remind your boss, yourself, and any other concerned party that you're all on the same team. You're all in the game to find the best way to work: the most productive and happiness-inducing setup wins. Hearing that pitch, only the most closed-minded are likely to continue digging in their heels.

What about culture?

Culture isn't a foosball table. It's not a paintball outing in the forest. It's not even the Christmas party where Steve got so drunk that everyone had a good story for the rest of the year. That's people hanging out and having a good time. No, culture is the spoken and unspoken values and actions of the organization. Here are a few examples:

- How we talk to customers—are they always right?
- What quality is acceptable—good enough or must it be perfect?
- How we talk to each other—with diplomatic tones or shouting matches?
- Workload—do we cheer on all-nighters or take Fridays off?
- Risk taking—do we favor bet-the-company pivots or slow growth?

Of course, that's partly a list of false dichotomies—most companies land somewhere in between. Nonetheless, you should know where *you* fall. The combination of all these values is what gives a company a certain feel, a certain culture.

Culture is incredibly important when it comes to

loosening the leash. The stronger the culture, the less explicit training and supervision is needed. In an ideal situation, managers-of-one are allowed to roam freely, it being understood that they'll do a good job—one congruent with what the company stands for.

You certainly don't need everyone physically together to create a strong culture. The best cultures derive from actions people actually take, not the ones they write about in a mission statement. Newcomers to an organization arrive with their eyes open. They see how decisions are made, the care that's taken, the way problems are fixed, and so forth.

If anything, having people work remotely forces you to forgo the illusion that building a company culture is just about in-person social activities. Now you can get on with the actual work of defining and practicing it instead.

I need an answer now!

When everyone is sitting in the same office, it's easy to fall into the habit of bothering anyone for anything at any time, with no regard for personal productivity. This is a key reason so many people get so little done in traditional office setups—too many interruptions. Still, when you're used to this mode of working, it can seem hard to envision a world where you can't get an answer to any question, no matter how insignificant, the second you think of it. Such a world does exist, though, and it's quite habitable.

First, it takes recognizing that not every question needs an answer immediately—there's nothing more arrogant than taking up someone else's time with a question you don't need an answer to right now. That means realizing that not everything is equally important.

Once you've grasped that, you're truly on the path to enlightenment and productivity. Questions you can wait hours to learn the answers to are fine to put in an email. Questions that require answers in the next few minutes can go into an instant message. For crises that truly merit a sky-is-falling designation, you can use that old-fashioned invention called the telephone.

With a graduated system like this, you'll quickly realize that 80 percent of your questions aren't so time-sensitive after all, and are often better served by an email than by walking over to someone's desk. Even better, you'll have a written record of the response that can be looked up later.

The next 15 percent can be handled in a chat or by instant message. Most people don't like to type that much in a chat anyway, so there's a tendency to get to the point. What would have been a lingering fifteen-minute interruption now turns into a three-minute ping-pong.

Finally, the last 5 percent can be dealt with over the phone. No, the body language doesn't carry over, but unless you're firing someone or conducting a difficult review, maybe that doesn't matter as much as you think.

Breaking your and others' addiction to ASAP won't come without withdrawal. You'll be frustrated the first couple days as your brain adjusts to matching interactions with others to the appropriate medium. You'll also have to resist the temptation to just transfer your expectations to a new medium you've chosen. Handling 80 percent of your questions with email won't work out well if you get upset when people don't answer within ten minutes.

Once you're ASAP-free, however, you'll be amazed at how your former self was able to get anything done in the face of constant in-person interruptions. It's almost zen-like to let go of the frenzy, to let answers flow back to you when the other party is ready to assist. Use that calm to be even more productive.

But I'll lose control

It's rarely spelled out directly, but a lot of the arguments against working remotely are based on the fear of losing control. There's something primal about being able to see your army, about having them close enough that you can shout "Now!!" like Mel Gibson did in *Braveheart*, and watch them pick up their spears in unison.

To a lot of people, being the big boss is about achieving such control. It's woven into their identity. To such alpha males and females, having someone under "direct supervision" means having them in their line of sight—literally. The thinking goes, *If I can see them, I can control them.*

Wresting that antiquated notion of control away from managers isn't a logical or rational process. It's often something that needs to be slow-walked—until the person calling the shots gets comfortable with the concept. In some ways it's similar to phobia therapy. You can't just tell someone who's afraid of spiders that their fear is silly and have them snap out of it. You have to work—one step at a time—to move the issue from the reptilian brain to the frontal lobe.

So if you're fighting against someone's fear of losing control, you have to start small and show that the world doesn't fall apart if you start working from home on Wednesdays. *Not only didn't it fall apart, but look at all this extra stuff I got done!* Then you can ramp it up to two days, and more flexible hours, and before you know it you're ready to move to another city and the wheels just keep on turning.

Well, it doesn't always work out like that. Even the best psychotherapists sometimes fail to cure arachnophobia, and you're probably not as thoroughly trained. But at least you know that your strategy is more likely to pay off than forcing the reptilian brain into fight or flight. If it's your boss, the choice will be fight, and you'll likely lose!

Because reptilian resistance is not rational but deeply emotional—even instinctual—the excuse "but I'll lose control" is the toughest to overcome. Even equipped with all the great arguments in this book, you may still fail. In that case, it just might be time to saddle up and consider another place to work.

We paid a lot of money for this office

This probably ranks up there as the most foolish excuse to forbid working remotely, but that hasn't prevented it from being aired from time to time. You really shouldn't even have to dignify such nonsense with a response, yet you just might have to, so here we go.

If someone has run a business well enough to be able to afford a fancy office, you'd think they'd be familiar with the idea of "sunk cost." But hey, we all look at the Kardashians and think, *How on earth did they get where they are?* Just summon that feeling, suspend your disbelief, and strap on your tweed blazer for a lesson in Business 101.

Sunk cost means that the money spent on the office is already spent. Whoever paid for it is not getting it back whether it's being used or not. So, rationally, the only thing that matters regarding where to work is whether the office is a more productive place or not. That's it.

If you want to get all mathematical about it, take out a napkin and jot down a few numbers. Say you can get five productive hours out of the office (ha!) and six productive hours out of working from home. That's 20 percent more productivity by working in your living room. Who's going to argue against that?

That wouldn't work for our size or industry

The easiest way to counter all the good arguments for remote work is to not even try. "Yeah, that sounds like a good idea in general, but it wouldn't work *for my* industry." Or "That's fine for small companies, but it won't scale." Oh really now.

Here's just a taste of some of the industries in which we found companies able to take advantage of remote work:

- Accounting
- Advertising
- Consulting
- Customer service
- Design
- Film production
- Finance
- Government
- Hardware
- Insurance
- Legal
- Marketing
- Recruiting
- Software

We aren't just talking about tiny fringe outfits in these industries either. In health insurance, Fortune 100 provider Aetna has nearly half of its 35,000 U.S. employees working from home. In accounting, Deloitte, which has about the same number of employees, has a staggering 86 percent working remotely at least 20 percent of the time. At Intel, 82 percent of their people regularly work remotely.

Even the government has gotten into the business of remote work. Eighty-five percent of the examiners of the U.S. Patent and Trademark Office, 57 percent of NASA's workers, and 67 percent of the Environmental Protection Agency's employees report that they work remotely to some extent.

Here's a small sample of companies at different scales doing remote work*

Companies with 10,000+ employees
- AT&T (Telecommunications)
- UnitedHealth Group (Healthcare)
- McKinsey & Co. (Consulting)
- Intel (Technology)
- S.C. Johnson & Son (Manufacturer)
- Aetna (Insurance)

---

* "Working Outside the Box," IBM white paper, 2009

- Cisco (Technology)
- Deloitte (Accounting)
- HSBC UK (Finance)
- British Telecom (UK Telecommunications)
- Unilever (Consumer Goods)
- Express Scripts (Pharmacy Benefit Management)

Companies with 1,000–10,000 employees
- Mercedes-Benz USA (Automotive)
- Teach For America (Education)
- Plante Moran (CPA, Business Advisory)
- DreamWorks Animation, SKG (Film Studio)
- Perkins Coie (Law)
- American Fidelity Assurance (Insurance)
- US Department of Education (Government)
- Virgin Atlantic (Airline)
- Brocade Communications (Technology)

Companies with less than 1,000 employees
- GitHub (Software)
- Ryan, LLC (Tax Services)
- Automattic (Web Development)
- MWW (Public Relations)
- Kony (Mobile App Development)
- TextMaster (Translations & Copywriting)
- BeBanjo (TV Software Supplier)

- Brightbox (Cloud Hosting)
- He:Labs (Web Development)
- Fotolia (Stock Imagery)
- FreeAgent (Online Accounting Software)
- Proof Branding (Branding & Design)

There really are very few industries left in which working remotely can categorically be ruled out. Don't let "industry fit" be the lame excuse that prevents remote work from happening at your company.

HOW TO COLLABORATE REMOTELY

Thou Shalt Overlap

Thou shalt overlap

Working remotely, if it is to be successful, usually requires *some* overlap with the hours your coworkers are putting in. Outsourcing gave remote working a bad reputation for many reasons, but one of the worst was that it could sometimes entail a full day's delay between communication or turnaround. Yes, working with such a delay is possible, but we don't recommend it. At 37signals, we've found that we need a good four hours of overlap to avoid collaboration delays and feel like a team.

That's not a problem if you're in Los Angeles working with someone in New York, but it's more of a challenge if, say, you're in Chicago working with someone in Copenhagen. That seven-hour time difference is something 37signals had to learn to cope with. There was no easy way around it; we just had to compromise. We did it with Copenhagen working from 11am to 7pm (local time) and Chicago working from 8am to 5pm—just enough for the key four hours of intersection.

Thankfully, there are lots of enjoyable work-life schedules outside the regular 9am to 5pm. Embrace that. Ironically, you'll probably get far more done when only half of your workday overlaps with the rest of your team. Instead of spending the entire day dealing with *Urgent!!!* emails and disruptive phone calls, you'll have the entire start (or end) of the day to yourself. Plus, you'd be surprised at how many people prefer unconventional work schedules. Maybe it gives them extra time for their family or hobbies, or they simply do their best work at night or crazy-early in the morning.

If there's just no getting around the time-zone issue—e.g., you find a superstar designer in Shanghai and you're in LA—well, you're probably going to have to work without a lot of real-time collaboration. That's not ideal; in fact, in most cases we think it's more of a challenge than it's worth—but some companies still manage to get it right when the payoff is big enough. (Saving money on labor is definitely not a valid reason to invite the hassle, but access to one-of-a-kind talent just might be.)

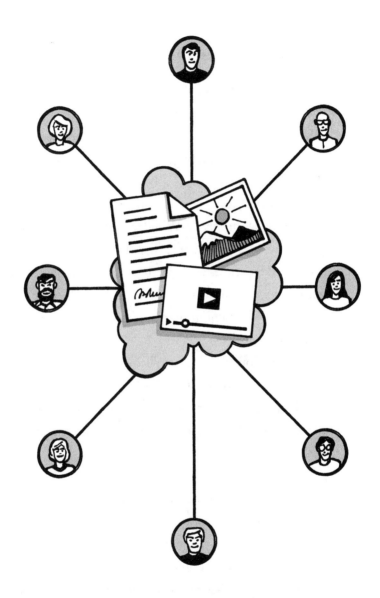

Seeing is believing

Some of the disdain toward working remotely is based on the fallacy that all remote collaboration happens blind-folded. We've all sat on a conference call and spent minutes describing something that would take seconds to show. It's *no bueno*.

Fortunately, it's an easy problem to fix. WebEx, Go-ToMeeting, Join.me, and similar tools all make it simple to share a screen. Use a shared screen to collaborate on everything from walking through a presentation, to going over the latest website changes, to sketching together in Photoshop, to just editing a simple text document together.

Before you know it, you'll be so used to sharing a screen that starting a call without one will feel pointless. Much of the magic that people ascribe to sitting together in a room is really just this: being able to see and interact with the same stuff.

Note that the type of screen sharing we're talking about is different from video conferencing, where the objective is to see each other's face. Screen sharing doesn't require a webcam—it's more like sitting next to each other in front of a computer or a projector. It's about collaborating on the work itself, not about reading facial expressions (although that too has a time and place).

This works just as well for asynchronous collaboration in slow time. When someone wants to demonstrate a new feature they're working on at 37signals, often the easiest way is to record a screencast and narrate the experience. A screencast is basically just a recording of your screen that others can play back later as a movie. It can be used in several ways, including for presenting the latest sales figures or elaborating on a new marketing strategy.

And if you're shaking your head right now bemoaning your lack of tech savvy, rest assured: this isn't just for techies—it's incredibly easy to do. On a Mac, screencast capability is built in: just start the QuickTime Player and select "New Screen Recording." Show what you want to show, narrate the experience using the computer's microphone, and voilà, everyone will be on the same page about what you've been working on.

Don't worry about trying to make it perfect, either. Screencasts can easily turn into a time suck if you try to make them Oscar-worthy or without a single mistake. Just let the tape roll and it'll be more than "good enough."

All out in the open

What do I have to do next? Where are the files for the pitch tomorrow? Is Jonas free to work on this with me next week? Do you have the email from Scott with the new mockups? These are all questions that rarely spark a second thought when we sit next to each other and work the same hours. Once you go remote, you're in for a wild goose chase, though, if the workflow and structure haven't been set up right.

Here's the key: you need everything available to everyone at all times. If Pratik in London has to wait five hours for someone in Chicago to come online in order to know what he should work on next, that's half a workday lost. A company won't waste time like that for long before declaring that "remote working just doesn't work."

As we talked about earlier, this problem of materials and instructions being out of reach is almost entirely solvable by technology. (The rest is a culture of good communication.) In fact, this very problem is why we originally created Basecamp, our first product. Basecamp gave us a single, centralized place in the sky to put all the relevant files, discussions, to-do lists, and calendars that keep the workflow ticking. It's what made it possible for us to grow the team from the original gang of four to thirty-six.

We pair Basecamp with GitHub, a code depository, so that all our code is available at all times to everyone, including change suggestions that can be discussed in slow time—over a couple of hours or days—as programmers comment on the thread.

We also use a shared calendar, so we know when Andrea's coming back from maternity leave or Jeff's going on vacation. If your company is too large to share one calendar, break it up by teams.

There are countless tools available these days to ensure everything is out in the open for your team. Some companies manage simply by using Dropbox to share files. Others use such products as Highrise or Salesforce to follow up on sales leads.

The point is to avoid locking up important stuff in a single person's computer or inbox. Put all the important stuff out in the open, and no one will have to chase that wild goose to get their work done.

The virtual water cooler

Working remotely can provide a terrific boost to productivity. Fewer interruptions, more work done! But all work and no play makes Jack a dull boy. Eight hours straight of work is not the utopia managers might think it is. We all need mindless breaks, and it helps if you spend some of them with your team. That's where the virtual water cooler comes in.

At 37signals, we use a chat program we created called Campfire. Other techy shops use IRC servers to achieve the same. The idea is to have a single, permanent chat room where everyone hangs out all day to shoot the breeze, post funny pictures, and generally goof around. Yes, it can also be used to answer questions about work, but its primary function is to provide social cohesion.

The wonderful thing about a chat room is that it doesn't require constant attention. People check in and check out during the day at natural break points. Did you just finish designing that screen? Awesome. Celebrate by posting a funny picture of a cat clapping and play the vuvuzela sound. You'll surely find a few coworkers who hadn't seen that particular cat before and bring some delight to their day.

But if cat pictures aren't your thing, a chat room can also be a great way to discuss news, the latest episode of

Game of Thrones, what you plan to eat for lunch—the same things that are discussed around the water cooler in the office. It's also a neat way to have a shared experience around live events. Our chat room is always buzzing when Apple has one of its big announcements.

This means that you, the remote worker, are in control of your social interaction—when it happens and how much of it you need. At first it might simply seem like a waste of time, especially if you're not already used to reading Reddit on the side, but it's a quality waste of time with your coworkers. We all need that.

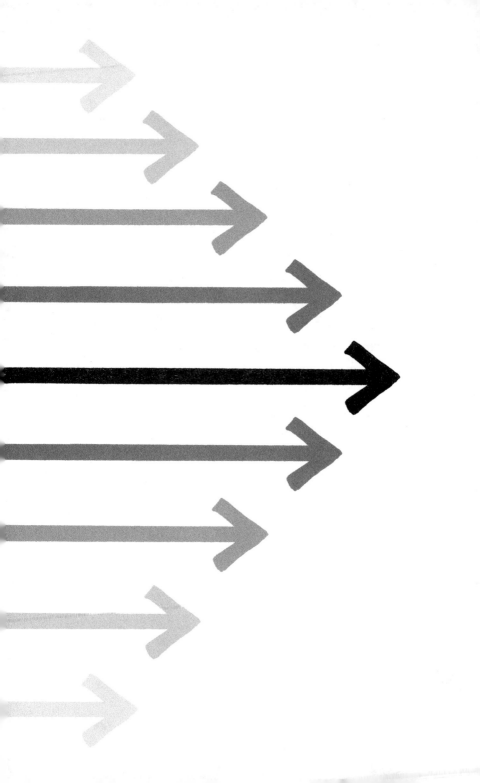

Forward motion

When you and your coworkers are sitting in the same place, it's easy to feel that you're up to speed on what's going on in the company. You stop and chat with office mates while making coffee in the morning, and over lunch you discuss the latest progress. There's just a constant, even *tacit* flow of information running through the office. Or at least it feels like that, and that feeling is comforting.

Working remotely doesn't automatically create that flow. Sure, there might be a project manager who checks in with everyone via email or chat, but that just gives *her* an idea what's going on. To instill a sense of company cohesion and to share forward motion, *everyone* needs to feel that they're in the loop.

At 37signals we've institutionalized this through a weekly discussion thread with the subject "What have you been working on?" Everyone chimes in with a few lines about what they've done over the past week and what's intended for the next week. It's not a precise, rigorous estimation process, and it doesn't attempt to deal with coordination. It simply aims to make everyone feel like they're in the same galley and not their own little rowboat.

It also serves as a friendly reminder that we're all in it

to make progress. Nobody wants to be the one to report that "this week was spent completing Halo 4, eating left-over pizza, and catching up on *Jersey Shore*." We all have a natural instinct to avoid letting our team down, so when that commitment becomes visual, it gets reinforced.

It's also a lot harder to bullshit your peers than your boss. In talking to a project manager without tech chops, programmers can make a thirty-minute job sound like a week-long polar expedition, but if their tall tale is out in the open for other programmers to see, it won't pass the smell test.

Simply put, progress is a joy best shared with co-workers.

The work is what matters

One of the secret benefits of hiring remote workers is that the work itself becomes the yardstick to judge someone's performance.

When you can't see someone all day long, the only thing you have to evaluate is the work. A lot of the petty evaluation stats just melt away. Criteria like "was she here at 9?" or "did she take too many breaks today?" or "man, every time I walk by his desk he's got Facebook up" aren't even possible to tally. Talk about a blessing in disguise!

What you're left with is "what did this person actually *do* today?" Not "when did they get in?" or "how late did they stay?" Instead it's all about the work produced. So instead of asking a remote worker "what did you do today?" you can now just say "*show* me what you did today." As a manager, you can directly evaluate the work—the thing you're paying this person for—and ignore all the stuff that doesn't actually matter.

The great thing about this is the clarity it introduces. When it's all about the work, it's clear who in the company is pulling their weight and who isn't.

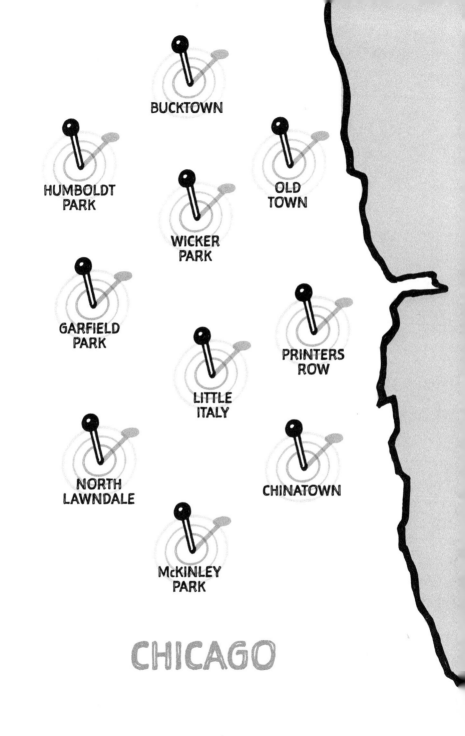

Not just for people who are out of town

Remote work isn't just for people who are out of town, across state lines, or on different continents. You can work remotely from down the street. Remote just means you're not in the office 9am–5pm, all day long.

At 37signals, thirteen people work out of our Chicago office. Or, more accurately, thirteen people have desks. It's a very rare day that all thirteen people are at the office. Most of the time it's just five or six. The others are working—just remotely.

And in this case, remotely might mean down the street at a coffee shop. Or at home. Or at the library. Or in a coworking space downtown. Yes, technically they're close by, but if they aren't in the office, they're as far away as an employee in Phoenix, New York, or Moscow.

If you're an owner or manager, letting local people work remotely is a great first step toward seeing if remote will work for you. It's low risk, it's no big deal, and worse comes to worst, people can start working at the office again.

But here's the thing: if you're going to give it a shot, give it a real shot. Try it for at least three months. There's going to be an adjustment period, so let everyone settle into their new rhythm. You can even start with two days remote, three days in the office. Then, if all goes well, flip it—two days in the office, three days remote. Work up to a full week out of the office.

This practice will provide the conditioning you need prior to hiring your first truly remote (read: far away) employee. You'll be prepared, you'll know what to expect, and you'll have a successful experiment under your belt.

Disaster ready

In systems design there's the notion of a Single Point of Failure, or SPoF. Much of the work required to achieve high reliability goes into finding and removing SPoFs. Everything eventually breaks, so if you don't have a backup system, it means you'll be out of commission.

Forcing everyone into the office every day is an organizational SPoF. If the office loses power or Internet or air conditioning, it's no longer functional as a place to do work. If a company doesn't have any training or structure to work around that, it means it's going to be unavailable to its customers.

This is even more of an issue in places likely to get hit by severe weather or natural disasters. Think of the snowstorms and hurricanes that pound the East Coast, the tornados that sweep through Kansas, the fires that plague Southern California—and that's just a few examples in the United States. There are natural disaster zones all around the world. Yet people still do business there.

American Fidelity Assurance (AFA) cited the ability to continue helping customers even during disasters as a key reason they're sticking with remote work. When they needed to close their headquarters in Oklahoma City for inclement weather, their remote workers all worked from home and customers never knew the difference.

Additionally, AFA employees who do not otherwise work remotely are asked to do so at least once or twice per month so they'll be ready if they have to during a disaster. The company also encourages everyone to stay home during the peak of flu season or during scares like H1N1.

Of course, while natural disasters are infrequent, personal "disasters" strike with regularity, and at such times the ability to work remotely is essential. In the traditional office scenario, your day is shot if you catch a cold, your child is sick, you have a plumbing issue that requires someone be home to greet the repairman, or any of the other myriad issues that might keep you from leaving the house but not necessarily unable to work.

Being in the routine of remote work helps you deal with these annoyances with less hassle. Whatever the world throws at it, be it a blizzard or the requirement to be home for the exterminator, a distributed workforce is one that can keep working regardless.

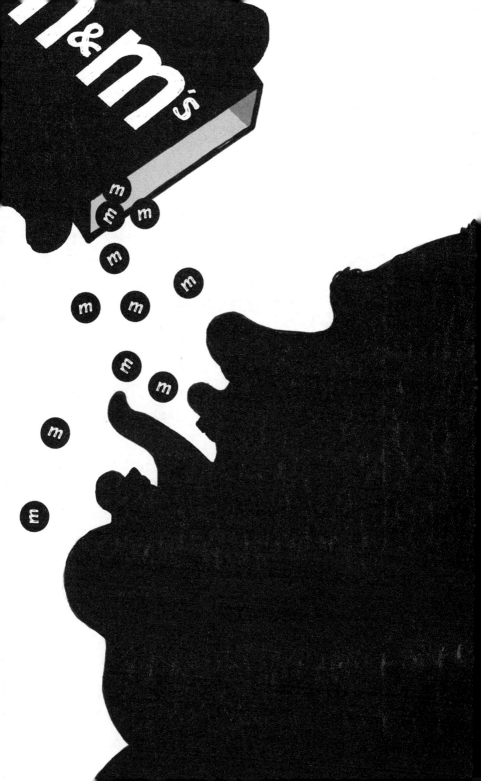

Easy on the M&Ms

Most of the time when you hear people imagining why remote work won't work, they'll point to two things in particular: One, you can't have face-to-face meetings when people aren't in the office. And two, managers can't tell if people are getting work done if they can't see them working.

We'd like to offer a very different perspective on these two points. We believe that these staples of work life—meetings and managers—are actually the greatest causes of work *not* getting done at the office. That, in fact, the further away you are from meetings and managers, the more work gets done. This is one of the key reasons we're so enthusiastic about remote work!

What exactly is wrong with meetings and managers (or M&Ms, as we call them)? Well, there's nothing *intrinsically* wrong with them. What's wrong is how often they're applied in office situations.

Meetings. Ah, meetings. Know anyone out there who wishes they had more meetings? We don't either. Why is that? Meetings should be great—they're opportunities for a group of people sitting together around a table to directly communicate. That should be a good thing. And it is, but only if treated as a rare delicacy.

When meetings are the norm, the first resort, the go-to tool to discuss, debate, and solve every problem, they become overused and we grow numb to the outcome. Meetings should be like salt—sprinkled carefully to enhance a dish, not poured recklessly over every forkful. Too much salt destroys a dish. Too many meetings can destroy morale and motivation.

Further, meetings are major distractions. They require multiple people to drop whatever it is they're doing and instead do something else. If you're calling a meeting, you better be sure pulling seven people away from their work for an hour is worth seven hours of lost productivity. How often can you say that a given meeting was worth it? Remember, there's no such thing as a one-hour meeting. If you're in a room with five people for an hour, it's a five-hour meeting.

Now what about managers? Managers are good. They're essential. But management, like meetings, should be used sparingly. Constantly asking people what they're working on prevents them from actually doing the work they're describing. And since managers are often the people who call the meetings, their very presence leads to less productive workdays.

Part of the problem is the perceived need to fill a whole day with management stuff, regardless of whether it's called for or not. All those dreaded status meetings, interruptions for estimates, and planning sessions have a curious way of adding up exactly to a manager's work-week. While monitoring output is sometimes quite important, it's rarely a forty-hour-per-week position. Ten hours maybe, but few full-time managers have the courage to limit their presence to that.

Working remotely makes it easier to spot managers drumming up busywork for themselves and others. The act of pulling people into a conference room or walking to their desks leaves no evidence of interruption, and it's all of the synchronous "drop what you're doing right now to entertain me!" variety. But when management is forced to manage remotely using email, Basecamp, IM, and chat, its intervention is much more purposeful and compressed, and we can just get on with the actual work.

M&Ms continue to have a place in the remote-working world, but you'll be more conscious about how many you consume when everything has a paper trail online. That's a good thing. We can all do with fewer M&Ms.

BEWARE THE DRAGONS

Cabin fever

Hell might be other people, but isolation sure ain't heaven. Even the most introverted are still part of Home-ous Socialitus Erectus, which is why prisoners fear The Hole more than living with other inmates. We're simply not designed for a life of total solitude.

The occasional drawback of working remotely is that it can feel like you're surrounded by plenty of people. You have your coworkers on instant messenger or in Camp-fire, you receive a constant deluge of emails, and you enjoy letting the trolls rile you up on Reddit. But as good as all that is, it's not a complete substitute for real, live human interaction.

Fortunately, one of the key insights we've gained through many years of remote work is that human inter-action does *not* have to come from either coworkers or others in your industry. Sometimes, even more satisfying interaction comes from spending time with your spouse, your children, your family, your friends, your neighbors: people who can all be thousands of miles away from your office, but right next to you.

But even if you don't have friends or family nearby, you can still make it work; you'll just have to exert a little more effort. For example, find a co-working facility and share desks with others in your situation. Such facilities can now be found in most larger cities, and even some smaller ones.

Another idea is to occasionally wander out into the real world. Every city, no matter how small, offers social activities to keep you sane and human, whether it's playing chess in the park, finding a pickup basketball game, or volunteering at a school or library on your lunch break.

Cabin fever is real, and remote workers are more susceptible to it than those forced into an office. Fortunately, it's an easy problem to address. Remote work doesn't mean being chained to your home-office desk.

Check-in, check-out

"Freedom is slavery," wrote George Orwell in his novel *1984*. Let's completely misappropriate that iconic banner and apply it to what happens to remote work if you don't manage the work-life balance correctly. That can happen, because when you're set free from punching in at 9am and out at 5pm, it's easy to don the shackles of working around the clock.

It starts innocently enough. You wake up by opening your laptop in bed and answering a few work emails from last night. Then you make yourself a sandwich and work through lunch. After dinner, you feel the need to check in with Jeremy on the West Coast about that one thing. Before you know it, you've stretched the workday from 7am to 9pm.

That's the great irony of letting passionate people work from home. A manager's natural instinct is to worry about his workers not getting enough work done, but the real threat is that *too* much will likely get done. And because the manager isn't sitting across from his worker anymore, he can't look in the person's eyes and see burnout.

What a manager needs to establish is a culture of reasonable expectations. At 37signals, we expect and encourage people to work forty hours per week on average.

There are no hero awards for putting in more than that. Sure, every now and then there's the need for a short sprint, but, most of the time, the company is viewing what it does as a marathon. It's crucial for everyone to pace themselves.

One way to help set a healthy boundary is to encourage employees to think of a "good day's work." Look at your progress toward the end of the day and ask yourself: "Have I done a good day's work?"

Answering that question is liberating. Often, if the answer is an easy "yes," you can stop working feeling satisfied that something important got accomplished, if not entirely "done." And should the answer be "no," you can treat it as an off-day and explore the Five Whys[*] (asking why to a problem five times in a row to find the root cause).

It feels good to be productive. If yesterday was a good day's work, chances are you'll stay on a roll. And if you can stay on a roll, everything else will probably take care of itself—including not working from when you get up in the morning until you go to sleep.

---

[*] http://en.wikipedia.org/wiki/5_Whys

Ergonomic basics

Working from home gives you the freedom to work wherever you want. Maybe you start at the kitchen counter, continue on the couch, and, if the weather is nice and you have a garden, finish up outside while enjoying the sunshine. But if you're going to make a real go at working from home for the long term, you'll need to get the ergonomic basics right.

That means getting a proper desk (height adjustable?), a proper chair (Humanscale Liberty?), and a proper screen (27 inches in high resolution!). All that stuff can seem expensive, but it's a great bargain if it means not ruining your back, your eyesight, or any other part of your anatomy.

At Accenture, where 81 percent of employees work remotely to some extent, they even have an internal process for this called "Ergonomics for Professionals" to ensure employees get it right. The company offers a list of equipment that's been picked for ergonomic comfort. It also offers the support of a certified ergonomics expert (an actual doctor!) who can work with people to find the best setup.

Unlike at your company headquarters, where some interior decorator picked out the same desk and chair for everyone, at home you can completely personalize your space. Maybe a chair isn't your thing. We have employees who work standing up, leaning on stools, sitting on exercise balls, and alternating between all of the above.

In fact, variation is often preferable to adopting a single style. Your body wasn't built to stay in the same position for eight hours a day, but it's hard to switch things around in most normal office settings.

And let's not forget the ergonomics of sweatpants! When you don't have to dress to impress, there's no shame in indulging your inner slob—at least part of the time. Just remember to change before venturing out into the real world for lunch.

Mind the gut

Modern office culture has never been conducive to a healthy lifestyle. Get up in the morning, commute to work, sit in a chair for eight hours, then return home to the couch and TV—no wonder people have been getting fatter.

But it can get worse! If you're not making a conscious effort to the contrary, working from home will likely afford even *less* opportunity to hit your recommended 10,000 steps per day.* At least, by traveling to an office, you have to walk to your car or to the train station or, even better, ride your bicycle. And, of course, in a conventional office, everyone walks around a little, seeking out those in other departments. And there's always the dash across the street to lunch, and maybe even some steps logged on the way home. (Studies vary, but office workers on average take between two and four thousand steps per day.)

You're certainly not going to turn into a model of fitness by being the average office worker. But how many steps do you think you get stumbling out of bed and into

---

* "The Pedometer Test: Americans Take Fewer Steps," *New York Times*, http://well.blogs.nytimes.com/2010/10/19/the-pedometer-test-americans-take-fewer-steps/

your home office in the next room? You'd probably be scared to strap on a pedometer to find out.

This very real problem was confirmed by the health insurance company Aetna, which has nearly half its 35,000 U.S. employees working from home. They discovered that the remote-working half tended to be heavier. Now they offer online personal trainers to help employees stay in shape.*

At 37signals, we try our best to encourage our remote workers to adopt a healthy lifestyle. Everyone gets a $100 monthly stipend for a health club membership, and we cover the cost of weekly fresh fruit and vegetable deliveries from local farmers.†

If there aren't built-in reasons to move during your day, find excuses to move—for example, instead of just eating lunch at your desk, walk to a café or sandwich shop. Take your dog for a long walk. Use a break to run on your treadmill. Now that you've saved time by skipping the commute, there really is no excuse for not finding the minutes to exercise or cook healthy meals.

---

* "For Some, Home = Office," *Wall Street Journal*, December 20, 2012
† "37vegetables," http://37signals.com/svn/posts/3151

The lone outpost

Here's how to guarantee a remote-work failure: Pick one employee who gets to "give this remote thing a try," then just carry on with business as usual. Three months later, mourn how it just didn't work out for your organization. "Jim simply wasn't connected enough anymore."

Well, duh.

You can't experiment with working remotely by sending one or two people to Siberia. To give it a proper try, you need to set free at least an entire team—including project management and key stakeholders! And then you need to give it longer than it takes to break in a new pair of shoes.

This is true even if you're surrounded by people who are wildly enthusiastic about working remotely (initially, most won't). It simply takes time to break old habits and get accustomed to new ways. When you're used to interrupting anyone any time you want, there'll be severe withdrawal symptoms when you can't.

There'll be days when you hate it, your boss hates it, and everyone else you're working with hates it. Just like there are days working at the office where you wish you could just turn everyone else into silent garden gnomes, so you can get a little work done. No work arrangement is without trade-offs.

The important thing is that everyone—or at least a sizable group—feels those trade-offs together. Otherwise, it's too easy just to focus on the negatives. When everyone else is still at the office, how will they appreciate the time you're not wasting in traffic, or the extra hours you're spending with your children, reading, or whatever you enjoy? They can't.

At American Fidelity Assurance, they launched their remote-work experiment with a team they felt was a natural fit—a pilot group. They made sure all technology and infrastructure was in place before rolling out the program to the whole company. And those in the pilot group became "company advocates" for remote work, sharing their success stories with their coworkers. In doing so, they pointed out how much their productivity had soared from increased morale. (The gain was so significant that an open position was closed since it was no longer needed.)

Give remote work a real chance or don't bother at all. It's okay to start small, but make sure it's meaningful.

☑ REMOTE
☑ REFERENCES
☑ SHOW WORK
☑ AVAILABLE
☑ PARTNERS

Working with clients

Before we were a software company, we were a website design consulting company. Companies would hire us to redesign their existing sites, or, occasionally, build them an entirely new site from scratch. We did this work from 1999 until around 2005. And we did it for dozens and dozens of clients—from massive corporations such as HP, Microsoft, and Getty to very small companies.

But here's the thing: Out of the dozens and dozens of clients we had, we only met a small handful. Most were based thousands of miles away. And we rarely got on an airplane to say hi and shake hands. We worked remotely.

All this work resulted in millions of dollars in fees. Yet we were just a small web design firm with a funny name ("37signals") based in Chicago.

What's the secret?

There isn't a secret. But we do have some tips. First, when pitching businesses, let the prospective client know up front that you don't live where they live. You want to begin building trust right at the beginning. You don't want to drop the line "Oh yeah, we won't be able to regularly meet with you face-to-face every week 'cause we're in Chicago and you're in Los Angeles" right before you sign the contract.

Second, provide references before the client even

asks. Show right up front that you have nothing to hide. Trust is going to be the toughest thing to build early on, so make it as easy as possible for the client to get to know your character by letting them speak with other clients— especially other clients who may be remote.

Third, show them work often. This is the best way to chip away at a client's natural situational anxiety. Look, they're paying you big bucks for your work, and it's totally natural for them to begin feeling anxious the moment they send you the deposit. So show them what they're paying for. When they see the results of your efforts, they'll feel a lot better about the relationship.

Fourth, be *very* available. Since you can't meet face-to-face, you better return phone calls, emails, instant messages, etc. This is basic business stuff, but it's tenfold more important when you're working remotely. It may be irrational but, if you're local, the client often feels that, if worse comes to worst, they can knock on your door. They "know where you live." But when you're remote, they're going to be more suspicious when phone calls go unreturned or emails keep getting "lost." Stay on top of communications and you'll reap the benefits.

Lastly, get the client involved and let them follow along. Make sure they feel that this is *their* project too. Yes, they're hiring you for your expertise, but they have plenty of their own. Set up a space online where you can use a shared schedule, show them work in progress, ask them for feedback, listen to their suggestions, and assign them some tasks (or let them assign some to you). When they feel part of the project, their anxieties and fears will be replaced by excitement and anticipation.

Taxes, accounting, laws, oh my!

"Is working remotely even legal?" is a common question. The answer is "yes"—but you have to be careful with the implementation. Labor laws can be a tangled web, and exposing yourself to undue liability is never a good idea.

In the United States, people can work remotely from anywhere in the country. Same city, different city. Same state, different state. At home sometimes, at the office sometimes. It's all okay. There are, however, some accounting concerns you should be aware of if you run a company and have remote workers outside your company's home state. A key concern is whether having a remote worker out of state establishes a "nexus" for your company (the legal term for having a taxable presence in the state). Having a nexus can lead to paying additional taxes in that state. And in some cases it could lead to your having to charge sales tax on sales to customers in that state. It's best to consult a qualified lawyer and an accountant to make sure you're properly set up.

It's slightly more complicated when you have an employee working in another country. This is where things can get a bit hairy, but the problem is by no means insurmountable. Fundamentally, there are two ways to hire people internationally: establish a local office or hire people as contractors. It's both expensive and slow to establish a local office, and it guarantees you'll have to deal with a taxation nexus. You'll need to retain lawyers and tax consultants to do it entirely by the book (which will likely cost you a small fortune). If you're going to hire dozens of people in a single country, there's probably no way around it, though.

Fortunately, most of the time you don't have to start with the Golden Gate when a simple suspension bridge will get you across the river. That is, it's probably best just to start out hiring people as contractors.

Every country has its own legal maze to complete to be perfectly legal when it comes to contractors, but the broad strokes are usually pretty similar. To qualify as a contractor, someone has to work on self-directed work (a firm can certainly argue this for writers, designers, programmers, consultants, analysts, etc., but it might be harder for a role such as personal assistant). The person contracted either has to have incorporated him or herself or be otherwise recognized as a company in their own right, so that they can send invoices. And they unfortunately can't partake in the regular regime of benefits offered to local employees. (That exclusion includes health care, but to cover that the contracting firm can always roll in additional compensation as part of the monthly invoice.)

This is also exactly how it works if you're a remote

worker wanting to work for a company in a foreign country. Set up that personal company and bill your "salary" as invoices every month. Most countries make it very easy to set up a personal company and, with such a simple invoice setup, taxation is not hard either. You'll have to consider which currency your invoice is going to be billed in, though. Most companies will want to pay in *their* currency, which means you carry the fluctuation risk—but as with anything in business, everything is negotiable.

So, to sum up, there's a little more work for the remote worker living in a different country, and there's a little more work for the company that is hiring them. And technically, whether you're a company owner or a worker, you *are* kinda running with scissors if you don't hire an army of experts to cross every "t" on the arrangement. But enterprising companies do this all the time and so do we at 37signals. It's worth the risk to have access to the best people in the world.

Of course, if you're *not* inclined to run with scissors, you can always hire some of the many lawyers and accountants who specialize in this stuff. Don't let a little work up front scare you away from the idea of remote working. The long-term benefits are worth it.

HIRING
AND KEEPING
THE BEST

CHICAGO

RIO

LONDON

COPENHAGEN

TOKYO

VLADIVOSTOK

It's a big world

When as an employer your eyes first open to the advantages of remote work, it's natural not to think outside your home country—especially if you're in the United States, or other large countries. The thought runs through your head: *Wouldn't it be too much of a hassle to hire someone from London if we can find someone from Portland almost as good to work with us in New York?* Not really.

37signals rose from that grander, international horizon. With David in Copenhagen and Jason in Chicago, the distance wasn't just cross-state; it was cross-continent. We've continued that trend over the years, happily finding and hiring talent from all over the world.

The bulk of the hassle in adjusting to remote work exists as soon as you're not sitting in the same office. The difference then between sitting in the same city, the same coast, or even the same country is negligible. Once you've formed good remote working habits, the lack of proximity between coworkers will start mattering so little that you'll forget exactly where people *are*. Nobody noticed much of a difference when Anton was working from Thailand instead of Russia. And we keep forgetting what city Jeremy is currently living in (it's somewhere on the West Coast). It just doesn't matter.

Thinking internationally when it comes to worker

recruitment doesn't just drastically increase the size of the talent pool; it also makes you better fit for tackling global markets. In software, for example, it helps you catch all those little things—like the calendar week starting on Sunday in the United States, but on Monday in much of the rest of the world. That's pretty important if you're designing a digital calendar.

International exposure can also serve as a selling point with clients. Alex Carabi, founder of Carabi + Co., a web design studio, lives and works in Copenhagen, Denmark, and Stockholm, Sweden, but purposely hires remote workers in other parts of the world because he feels having an international team helps him win clients. Having input from Texas, London, and Auckland, New Zealand, contributes to a wider range of ideas and perspectives.

As we've already pointed out, hiring around the world is not without complication, though. For one thing, as we discussed in "Thou shalt overlap," you have to ensure that the time zones work. It's also important to know the legal and accounting ramifications, as we covered in "Taxes, accounting, laws, oh my!"

On top of all that, be mindful of language barriers. With remote work, most communication is written. Many people who can get by with so-so language skills in the spoken realm fall flat when it comes to the written word. There simply isn't much room for weak communication on teams with tight collaboration. You need solid writers to make remote work work, and a solid command of your home language is key.

The world has never been smaller and markets have never been more open. Don't be a cultural or geographical hermit.

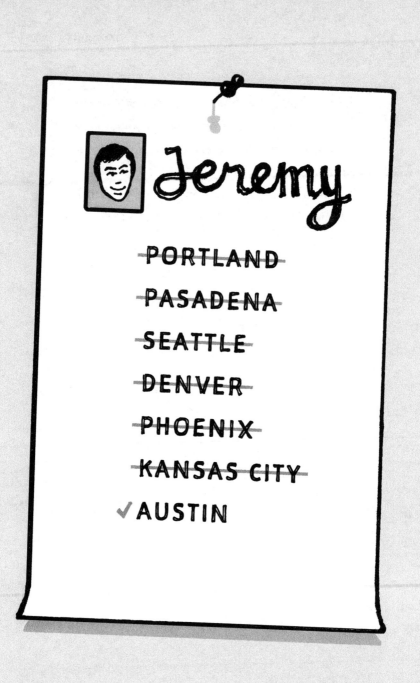

Life moves on

Given how hard it is to find great people, you should be doing your utmost to keep them. That sounds self-evident, yet plenty of companies are willing to let their stars disappear when life forces them to move. That's just plain dumb.

There are myriad reasons why people have to—or want to—move, even if they love their job. Among them: they get married (or divorced), they grow tired of the snow (or extreme heat), they want to be closer to family, or they just want a fresh scene. None of this has anything to do with work, but the fixation that most companies have on keeping their workers within a literal arm's reach means it quickly will.

As it turns out, people who've been with a company for a long time make ideal remote workers. They already know everyone, how everything works, and what they need to do. Throwing away all that knowledge and good spirit is not only dumb, it's expensive. No matter how well qualified a candidate, nobody will hit the ground running like the person who's been in the position for years and proven their mettle.

In the many years 37signals has been in business, its practice of holding on to migrating workers has succeeded beautifully. David has moved from Chicago to

Marbella, Jamis from Utah to Idaho, Kristin from Chicago to Portland, and Jeremy has lived in Portland, Pasadena, San Diego, and Phoenix, all while working for the company.

In the case of Jellyvision, it was actually a star employee's desire to move that put them on the remote working track. The employee's spouse landed a dream job that required her to move out of state. The employee didn't want to leave Jellyvision, and they didn't want him to go either. To this day, most of company's remote employees started at headquarters but then decided to move away from Chicago secure in the knowledge that Jellyvision would want to keep them in the fold.

At American Fidelity Assurance, they were confronted with a similar situation—a valued employee wanting to move but on a temporary basis. She moved from the company's headquarters in Oklahoma to Arkansas to be with her husband while he finished college, but she intends to move back once he's done.

Keeping a solid team together for a long time is a key to peak performance. People grow closer and more comfortable with each other, and consequently do even better work. Meanwhile, rookie teams make rookie mistakes.

Remember, doing great work with great people is one of the most durable sources of happiness we humans can tap into. Stick with it.

Keep the good times going

It's tempting to think that if you don't have to sit next to someone every day, you can ignore all the social elements of hiring. All you need is a superhero worker who can crank out good stuff as fast as possible, right? Wrong. *Dead wrong.*

If anything, the human connection is even more important when hiring remote workers because it has to be stronger to survive the distance. When the bulk of your communication happens via email and the like, it doesn't take much for bad blood to develop unless everyone is making their best effort to the contrary. Small misunderstandings that could have been nipped in the bud with a wink of an eye or a certain tone of voice can quickly snowball into drama. That's one of the key challenges of remote work: keeping everyone's outlook healthy and happy. That task is insurmountable if you've stacked your team with personalities who tend to let their inner asshole loose every now and again.

Even for people with the best intentions, relations can go astray if the work gets stressful (and what work doesn't occasionally?). The best ballast you can have is as many folks in your boat as possible with a thoroughly optimistic outlook. We're talking about people who go out of their way to make sure everyone is having a good time.

Remember: sentiments are infectious, whether good or bad.

That's also why it's as important to continuously monitor the work atmosphere as to hire for it. It's never a good idea to let poisonous people stick around to spoil it for everyone else, but in a remote-work setup it's deadly.

When you're a manager and your employees are far flung, it's impossible to see the dread in their eyes, and that can be fatal. With respect to drama, it therefore makes sense to follow the "No Broken Windows" theory of enforcement.

What are we talking about? Well, in the same way that New York cracked down in the '90s on even innocuous offenses like throwing rocks through windows or jumping the turnstile, a manager of remote workers needs to make an example of even the small stuff— things like snippy comments or passive-aggressive responses. While this responsibility naturally falls to those in charge, it works even better if policed by everyone in the company.

Sometimes it just boils down to practice. As online accounting service FreeAgent learned: "Getting used to having deep, extensive discussions over email or Basecamp was tricky. Learning to get the tone of your messages right can be a challenge—it's all too easy to come across in the wrong way, especially when you haven't really got to know each other, and we did this all too frequently for a while."

The old adage still applies: No assholes allowed. But for remote work, you need to extend it to no asshole-y behavior allowed, no drama allowed, no bad vibes allowed.

Seeking a human

We make such a point of looking at the work that it's easy to forget the humans behind it. The way to turn out the best work is not to assemble a cadre of ninja robots who can work from dawn till dusk and think of nothing else. Smart solutions, friendly service, and edgy design all happen at the intersection of professional skill and life experience.

While you can do much to counter it, having people work remotely does carry the risk of narrowing their lives. It's the furthest thing from working on a big company campus, for example, with, potentially, a gym, a restaurant, even someone doing your laundry (as is not atypical in Silicon Valley). Plus, there's even the casual Friday happy hour. A worker searching for a diverse work experience may look at that and feel it's the finished package.

That sets a challenge for a manager directing a remote workforce. He has to ensure that this diversity of human experience happens for his troops as well. The job starts with putting together a team of people who are naturally interested in more than just their work— and it continues with encouraging those other interests to bloom.

At 37signals we actively sponsor such endeavors. The last two years, our holiday gift has been a selection of curated traveling experiences, such as a trip to a cooking school in Paris or an outing for the whole family to Disneyland—all intended to promote memorable experiences with family or friends, new places, new skills.

We've also sponsored the pursuit of a long list of hobbies and made sure that people get the time off to fit them in. Those hobbies include bicycle racing, whittling, trekking, motorsports, gardening, and many more. Sure, people working in an office have hobbies too, but few companies give their workers both the time off to pursue their hobbies and the financial support to make them affordable.

Magic and creativity thrive in diverse cultures. When you're seeking remote workers, you have to do even more to encourage and nurture diversity and personal development. It's a small price to pay for a more interesting workplace and to keep people engaged for the long term.

No parlor tricks

It's a recruiter's dream. If we could just give everyone a riddle or a quiz that would tell us whether they're smart or not, we wouldn't have to bother looking at their past work history or give them a test project.

In the 1990s, Microsoft was infamous for using all sorts of riddles and quizzes and other parlor tricks to separate the wheat from the chaff. The approach was ballyhooed in the book *How Would You Move Mount Fuji?*, which is subtitled *Microsoft's Cult of the Puzzle—How the World's Smartest Companies Select the Most Creative Thinkers.*

This method of identifying the best and the brightest is hogwash. The correlation between people who are really good at solving imaginary puzzles and people who best fit your company is likely to be tenuous at best, even with respect to engineering positions. And while there may well be *some* matches, there are likely to be far more false negatives.

There *is* a time and a place for using personality assessments, like those provided by companies such as Caliper (which do include logic aptitude sections). But the assessments are strictly there to remind you of traits you've already observed by meeting someone in person. (You didn't think you could get by without *ever* meeting them, did you? See "Meeting them in person" for more.)

All of these other parlor tricks are indirect measures of looking at a candidate—probably even less reliable than looking at their college grade point average. For most of the work that can be done remotely, it's entirely unnecessary to go the indirect route.

Instead, you can ask copywriters to show you copy, consultants to show you reports or results, programmers to show you code, designers to show you designs, marketers to show you campaigns, and so on and so forth.

This is an important aspect of recruiting in general, but it's even more important for hiring remote workers. The main way you'll communicate is through the work itself. If the quality just isn't there, it'll be apparent from the second the person starts—and you'll have wasted everyone's time by hiring on circumstantial evidence.

Asking to see work product is pretty easy for positions with natural portfolios, such as designer, programmer, or writer. For positions that don't lend themselves to portfolio accumulation, you can simply pose real-world problems and have the person answer them as part of the application.

For example, all the customer support people we hire answer one of the following questions as part of their application:

- Does the new Basecamp offer time tracking?
- Is the new Basecamp offered in any other language besides English?

- I'm interested in your products, but not sure which one is right for me. What's the difference between Highrise and Basecamp?
- I've been a Basecamp Classic user for years and see you have a new version. What's the difference between the versions, and why should I switch?

These are all real questions from real customers that a support person would face all the time on the job. The applicant might not know the answers to these questions off the top of their head before applying, but the queries are approachable enough that a little research into our products will reveal the answer.

You need this kind of real-world, real-work filter when you're sorting through a hundred résumés from a hundred different cities. Booking flights for in-person interviews with everyone who has an appealing-looking CV just doesn't scale.

It's the work that matters. Look at the work and forget the abstractions.

The cost of thriving

As a company owner looking for a way to reduce payroll, it's tempting to recruit from places with a lower cost of living. In some industries with low margins that approach may well be worth pursuing, but it's not the interesting part of remote working for most knowledge-based companies.

Instead of thinking *I can pay people from Kansas less than people from New York,* you should think *I can get amazing people from Kansas and make them feel valued and well-compensated if I pay them New York salaries.*

If your entire workforce is located in a hot hub and you pay market salaries, you'll be under constant attack from poachers. People are naturally more inclined to change jobs when it's a level playing field and the poacher's pay is higher.

Now compare this to hiring an ace customer support person from Fayetteville, Tennessee, or a star programmer from Caldwell, Idaho, or a design wiz from Edmond, Oklahoma, and paying them all big-city market salaries. It's going to be awfully hard for the employee to find a better deal at a local company (since they'll tend to pay local rates).

In fact, we actually hired all those people. In order, they are Chase Clemons, who's been with the company for two years; Jamis Buck, who's been with us for seven years; and Jason Zimdars, who's been with us for four years. In some industries, those tenures might not sound so long, but in technology they're an eternity.

These days few companies offer remote work (though, of course, the point of this book is that remote work is on the rise), and even fewer do so with equal pay for equal work across geographies. The ones that do are at an almost unfair advantage in attracting and keeping the best people in the world. So don't look at remote work as a way to skimp on salaries; you'll save on lots of other things. Your star designer out in the sticks is just as valuable (maybe more so) to the team as those working from the big-city home office. Make sure she feels that way.

By the same token, as a remote worker, you shouldn't let employers get away with paying you less just because you live in a cheaper city. "Equal pay for equal work" might be a dusty slogan, but it works for a reason. If with regard to compensation you accept being treated as a second-class worker based on location, you're opening the door to being treated poorly on other matters as well.

Great remote workers are simply great workers

It's a lot harder to fake your way as a remote worker. As the opportunities to schmooze in the office decrease, the focus on the work itself increases. Additionally, central online repositories for tracking tasks and reporting progress, like Basecamp, create an irrefutable paper trail showing what everyone is getting done and how long it's taking.

This gives back the edge to quiet-but-productive workers who often lose out in a traditional office environment. In a remote setup, you don't need to constantly boast about the quality of your stuff when it's already apparent to everyone willing to pay attention. Likewise, if you're all talk and no walk, it's painfully clear for all to see.

Remote work pulls back the curtain and exposes what was always the case, but not always appreciated or apparent: great remote workers are simply great workers. They exhibit the two key qualities, as Joel Spolsky labeled them in his "Guerrilla Guide to Interviewing".* Smart, and Gets Things Done.

---

* http://www.joelonsoftware.com/articles/GuerrillaInterviewing3.html

When the work product is out in the open, it's much easier to see who's *actually* smart (as opposed to who simply *sounds* smart). The collective judgment rarely even has to be verbalized. Conversely, if the work keeps getting flagged with problems, it's evidence that the Smarts aren't sufficiently present for the work at hand. Also, if the duration between installments of new work or tasks being checked off is persistently lengthy, it's a sign that the Gets Things Done bit is missing.

Both of these weaknesses are easier to miss when you see someone at the office every day. Especially if they're just generally a nice person. The mental shortcut usually goes: In the office from 9–5 + nice = must be a good worker.

Of course, someone who's either not smart enough for the job or doesn't get things done is always found out eventually. But since few people will tell on a colleague unless the problem is of serious magnitude, it's common to get stuck with lots of people who put in the hours and are plenty nice, but don't fit the criteria established for being a great worker.

Remote work speeds up the process of getting the wrong people off the bus and the right people on board.[*]

---

[*] "Who" before "what" from Jim Collins's "Good to Great": http://www.jimcollins.com/article_topics/articles/good-to-great.html

On writing well

Being a good writer is an essential part of being a good remote worker. When most arguments are settled over email or chat or discussion boards, you'd better show up equipped for the task. So, as a company owner or manager, you might as well filter for this quality right from the get-go.

This means judging an application by its cover . . . letter. Yes, the CV might list all sorts of impressive stints here, there, and everywhere, but let's be honest—it's usually embellished and not a great indicator of how the candidate will perform for your company.

No, the first filter that *really* matters is the cover letter explaining exactly why there's a fit between applicant and company. There's simply no getting around it: in hiring for remote-working positions, managers should be ruthless in filtering out poor writers.

Most applicants would probably be surprised if they knew *how* ruthless hiring managers are these days. We've had openings that have attracted 150 responses. How long do you think we spend going over applications with the big comb? Less than thirty seconds per application. Sometimes less than *ten* seconds.

When a manager has to whittle down 150 to maybe 10–15 for a second look, that's the only approach that works. And it's the writing in the cover letter that decides which applications live or die.

Thankfully, becoming a better writer is entirely possible. Few people are born with an innate talent for writing; most good writers have practiced and studied their way through. Besides, it's not as if you need to be Hemingway or Twain. But you *do* need to take it seriously.

You should read, read, and read some more. Study how good writers make their case. Focus on clarity first, style second. Here are a few books to start with if you're serious about becoming a better writer:

On Writing Well by William Zinsser
The Elements of Style by William Strunk and E. B. White
Revising Prose by Richard Lanham

Are there *any* remote workers who can get away without strong writing skills? Sure. If your work truly doesn't involve a lot of collaboration or back-and-forth, you might be able to get away with less-than-impeccable writing skills. There's a place for people who just excel at crunching numbers in solitude or sales people pummeling resistance through the phone. Good writing skills *still* help in those cases, but they can take a backseat to other great qualities.

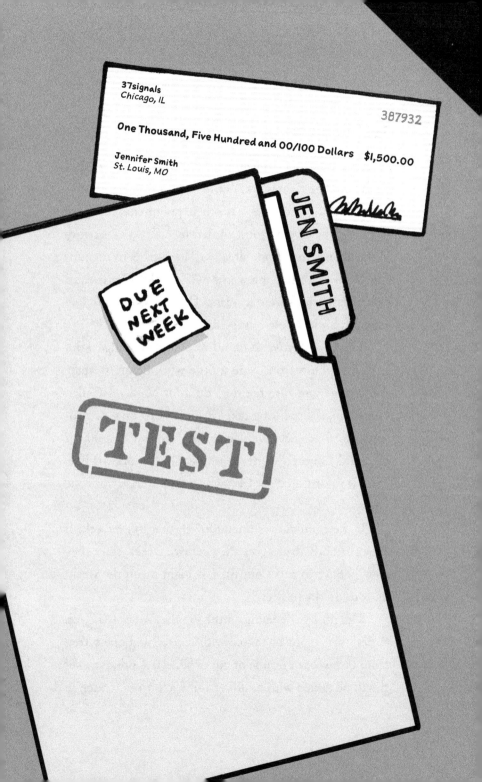

Test project

It doesn't matter if someone is local or remote—we still want to judge their work, not their résumé.

A lot of companies base their judgments on work already done. We do some of that too. But what's tricky about that is that work already done is hard to account for. Who *really* did the work? Was it solo? On a team? What limitations were in place? Did the work take way longer than it should have? Etc.

The best way we've found to accurately judge work is to hire the person to do a little work before we take the plunge and hire them to do a lot of work. Call it "pre-hiring." Pre-hiring takes the form of a one- or two-week mini-project. We usually pay around $1,500 for the mini-project. We never ask people to work for free. If *we* wouldn't do it for free, why would we ask someone else to do it?

If the candidate is unemployed, they get a week. If they currently have a job, they get two weeks, since they usually have to carve out time at night or on the weekends to do the project.

The project depends on the job they're applying for. A designer might be tasked with redesigning one screen from our website or one of our products. A programmer might be tasked with building a tiny app from scratch in a week. If you're hiring a writer, have them write something.

Whatever it is, make it meaningful. Make it about creating something new that solves a problem. We don't believe in asking people to solve puzzles. Solving real problems is a lot more interesting—and enlightening.

Meeting them in person

By now we know what it means to *work* remotely, but what does it mean to *hire* remotely? Do you hire remote workers the same way you hire local workers?

Assuming the person you're considering has met your basic qualifications for skills, competency, etc., the next step is figuring out if they're the right fit culturally. Even though they'll be working remotely, it makes sense, before making the final hiring decision, to meet them in person. This allows you to get a feel for their character. Are they polite? Do they show up on time? Are they fundamentally decent? Do they treat people well? What does the rest of the team think? You can tell a lot from a quick face-to-face.

What we usually do is narrow the field to about two or three final candidates. Then we'll fly each in for a day. Since we already know we like their skills (otherwise they wouldn't have gotten this far), the in-person meeting is to determine if we like the "person."

The meeting is informal—usually over lunch. And since we have a large part of the team in Chicago, we often let the candidate go out with their potential team coworkers instead of their manager. The prospective hire is going to be working with their teammates a lot more than their manager, so it's important that the team get a good feel for this person.

After the candidate gets back from lunch, they'll sit down with the manager, shoot the breeze a bit, and then they're invited to hang out at the office the rest of the day. They can work, observe, whatever. We want them to see if they feel comfortable with us, and we want to see if we feel comfortable with them.

After they're gone, we sit down with the team that took them to lunch and chat a bit. Were they nice? Would you want to work with this person? How did they treat the wait staff? Were they respectful? Would they fit in at 37signals? It's really up to their peers at this point.

If you don't have part of the team in the same city as the manager doing the in-person evaluation, you'll have to simulate the situation in other ways. Using a video chat system that allows for a whole group to be online together, like Google Hangouts, is a reasonable substitute. It won't be as good, but it'll do.

In the end, we make the call on talent and character. It's always a blend. If we offer them the job, and they want to work with us, we virtually shake hands and often invite them back to the office for their first few weeks on the job. This way they can get a bit more acclimated to the team, the culture, the faces, the names, etc. Once oriented, they can go back home with a solid introduction to the company, the people, and the way we work.

Contractors know the drill

If there's an ideal training regimen for remote workers, it's being a contractor for a while. As a contractor, you have to be able to set a reasonable schedule, show good progress at regular intervals, and convert an often fuzzy definition of the work into a deliverable. All these are skills perfectly suited for remote work.

Contract work is an excellent way for both the company doing the hiring and the person being hired to ease into remote work and try it on for size. In a sense, both sides are test driving each other. Part of the appeal of contract work is that if your client is a bozo, then at least you don't have to work with them forever. Once the contract is up, you're free to try another fish in the sea. But given how many stories most contractors have about bozo clients, it's not exactly a stretch to imagine them champing at the bit if they find a client who's not.

Someone who's had a chance to taste the dysfunction of several companies as a contractor is more likely to appreciate a company that actually *gets* remote work. Because of the trust needed and the good work practices required, a contractor can be fairly safe in assuming that a company cool with remote work is just cool in general.

CHAPTER

MANAGING
REMOTE WORKERS

BUSINESS START-UP TASKS

- ☑ Apply for an LLC
- ☑ Remote Working
- ☐ Create a Logo
- ☐ Build a Website
- ☐ Call on prospects
- First Project

When's the right time to go remote?

If I'm starting a new company today, should I start remote today? What if I already *have* a company? How do I begin including remote workers in a culture that is already well established?

In general, it's best if you start as early as possible. Cultures grow over time, and it'll be a lot easier if your culture grows up with remote workers. Think about kids born after computers arrived—they know computers really well because they grew up with them. Now compare that to your parents—they often struggle with computers because they were introduced late in life. Your company is the same. Start early.

That said, if you do have a company that's well established, you can always introduce remote workers to the mix. It won't be as easy, but lots of things that are worth doing aren't easy. It just takes commitment, discipline, and, most important, faith that it's all going to work out.

A great place to start is to allow your current employees to begin working remotely. You don't have to hire new people out of town to test this out—float the idea to some of your best employees. Tell them they can work from home a couple days a week if they'd like. We bet that at least a few will take you up on it.

If you treat remote work as a low-risk experiment,

you'll be able to iterate, adjust, and try a variety of things to see what works best. You may want to offer the remote option to people on different teams. Maybe it'll turn out that one type of job is easily done remotely, while another really feels as though it should happen in the office. You never know until you try.

So start early if you can, but if you can't, start small. Take a tiny step with a few trusted current employees. Let them work outside the office a couple days a week. See what happens. It's low risk and you'll immediately start learning whether the policy makes sense.

Stop managing the chairs

It's easy to be a manager when all you have to do is manage the chairs. Making sure that the little worker bees arrive by nine in the morning and giving them an extra star on their score card if they stay past six—this is how much of management has operated since forever. It's only through the determination of said worker bees that anything ever got done over the years, given such ludicrous measures of productivity.

Working remotely blows a big fat hole in that style of management. *If I can't see workers come in and leave their desks, how on earth can I make sure they're actually working?* Or so goes the naïve thinking of a manager of chairs. Thinking on it further, our naïve manager asks himself, *What is my managerial role at the company, if not to ensure that the workers are working?*

Elementary, Watson. The job of a manager is not to herd cats, but to lead and verify the work. The trouble with that job description is that it requires knowledge of the work itself. You can't effectively manage a team if you don't know the intricacies of what they're working on.

That doesn't mean every programming manager has to be a programmer (although it helps) nor that every design director has to design every screen (but again, it helps if they're able to). No, it means they should know what needs to be done, understand why delays might happen, be creative with solutions to sticky problems, divide the work into manageable chunks, and help put the right people on the right projects. Well, that and about a million other things that will ensure work proceeds with as little bother and as few obstacles as possible.

What's certain is that a clued-in manager does *not* need to manage the chairs. When or where someone is doing the work is irrelevant most of the time. Whether the copy is being written in London, the code implemented in Marbella, or the design drafted in Edmond really has no bearing on whether the copy is good, the code is right, the design a fit.

Meetups and sprints

Just because you don't have a permanent office, or not everyone is working out of one, that's no reason not to get together every now and then. In fact, it's almost mandatory to do so occasionally.

At 37signals, we meet up at least twice a year for four to five days. Part of the reason is to talk shop, present the latest projects, and decide the future direction of the company. But the bigger deal is to put moving faces with screen names, and to do it with enough regularity that we don't forget each other's in-person personalities.

The fact is, it's just easier to work remotely with people you've met in so-called "real life"—folks you've shared laughs and meals with. Meetups are especially important as a way to introduce new people to the rest of the team. Since we finished our nice new office in Chicago, we've held our meetups there, but in the past we've picked such places as Kohler, Wisconsin; San Diego, California; and York Harbor, Maine.

FreeAgent, headquartered in Edinburgh, Scotland, takes advantage of the fact that the world's largest festival of the arts is located there to bring people together every summer. Their eleven remote workers join up with the other thirty-nine FreeAgent employees who live there. Fotolia, a stock-photo company, employs eighty people with half working remotely across twenty-two countries. For their last meetup, they brought everyone to Marrakech, Morocco. Talk about an international spirit!

As important as it is to have the entire company get together, it's also a great idea to occasionally do a sprint with a smaller group to finish a specific project. If the company must make a mad dash to meet a deadline—with the unreasonable hours and pressure that implies—it can be nice to slave through the ordeal together.

We've done this in the past when we've launched a new product or finished a particularly gnarly feature in our software, or when people have simply wanted to top off on some social interaction.

Going to an industry conference is another good opportunity for team bonding. You'll learn something new together, and you usually have the evenings free to socialize.

Just because you work remotely most of the time doesn't mean you have to, or should, work remotely all of the time. Fill up the camel's back every now and then with some in-person fun.

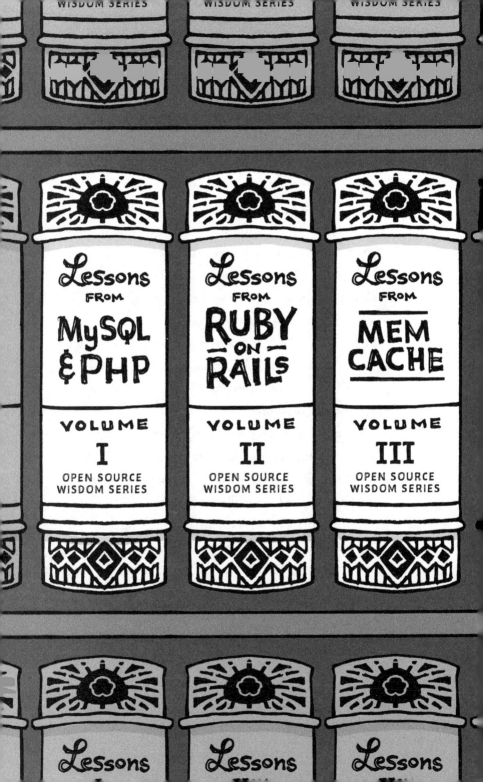

Lessons from open source

Would-be remote workers and managers have a lot to learn from how the open source software movement has conquered the commercial giants over the past decades. It's a triumph of asynchronous collaboration and communication like few the world has ever seen.

On its face, it sounds like an implausible mission. Building complex software is difficult enough as it is. It would seem prudent to try to remove all other sources of complication. Like, say, managing thousands of people spread out all over the globe, some even in rarely overlapping time zones (which can pose the greatest challenge to effective collaboration).

But as with much of intuitive knowledge, this too is simply wrong. From the operating system Linux to the MySQL database to the PHP language to Ruby on Rails, open source has spanked such behemoth commercial competitors as Microsoft, Oracle, and others.

Compared to your average business or consumer software package, all these open source examples are endlessly more complex and involve far more people in their production. If people can manage to build world-class operating systems, databases, programming languages, web frameworks, and many other forms of software while working remotely, you'd probably be wise to look more closely at how it's done.

If you look, for example, at Ruby on Rails, the web framework we created at 37signals, we've managed to evolve the code base for over a decade and have kept adding features and improving code quality. Close to 3,000 people from dozens of countries and hundreds of cities have contributed to that code base over time—and the vast majority have never met each other! Normally, the path goes like this in software development: old code + lots of new features + lots of different developers = big ball of spaghetti mud!

And yet it's worked. Hell, it's not only worked, it's succeeded beyond our wildest dreams and expectations. The key ingredients of this success follow much of the other advice in this book, but let's look at a few anyway:

- Intrinsic motivation: Programmers working on open source code usually do it for love, not money. Often the money follows, but rarely does it take the place of motivation. To translate: working on exciting problems you're personally interested in means you don't need a manager breathing down your neck and constantly looking over your shoulder.
- All out in the open: Much of open source is coordinated on mailing lists and code tracking systems like GitHub. Anyone who's interested in helping out *can* because the information is all out

in the open. You can self-select into participating, and the people with the most knowledge about an issue thus get easy access.

• Meeting occasionally: Most successful open source projects eventually grow to the point where they can support their own conferences or, at least, sessions at general ones. This gives contributors a chance to meet in person to top off on social interaction—much like meetups and sprints do for companies. But it's not a requirement, it's a nice-to-have.

So when in doubt or down about hitting a roadblock with remote work, just think, *At least I'm not trying to corral and merge the work of 3,000 people across the globe on a single project.* You'll instantly feel better about the modest scope of your problem.

Level the playing field

If you treat remote workers like second-class citizens, you're all going to have a bad time. The lower the ratio of remote worker to office worker, the more likely this is to happen. It's the normal dynamic and it won't get solved unless you tackle it head-on.

Feeling like a second-class worker doesn't take much. Case in point: a roomful of local people and a shitty intercom system that makes it hard for the remote worker to hear what's going on and even harder to participate. There's also the annoyance of having every debate end with "John and I talked about this in the office yesterday and decided that your idea isn't going to work." Fuck that.

As a company owner or manager, you need to create and maintain a level playing field—one on which those *in* and *out* of the office stand as equals. That's easier said than done, but one way to better your chances is to have some of the top brass working remotely. People with the power to change things need to feel the same hurt as those who merely *have* to deal with it.

When New York City's subway system was plagued by crime and vandalism in the 1990s, New York's Police Commissioner William Bratton forced his commanders to use the subway. When they saw with their own eyes how bad things were, change soon followed.

This doesn't mean managers have to move to another city to feel the same hurt. Just have them work from home a few days a week. They'll get at least some sense of what it's like to wear a remote worker's shoes. Even better, though, than having managers *occasionally* work from home is having them actually be remote. For example, Herman Miller, the Michigan-based manufacturer of office furniture, equipment, and home furnishings, employs as head of its design team Betty Hase, who from her office in Chicago reports to a boss in New York and oversees a team of ten located across the United States.

The mechanics of leveling the playing field are pretty simple: Get great intercom systems, use shared desktop apps like WebEx to ensure everyone is seeing the same thing while collaborating, and hold as many discussions as possible on email and other online messaging platforms. Above all, think frequently about how you'd feel as a remote worker.

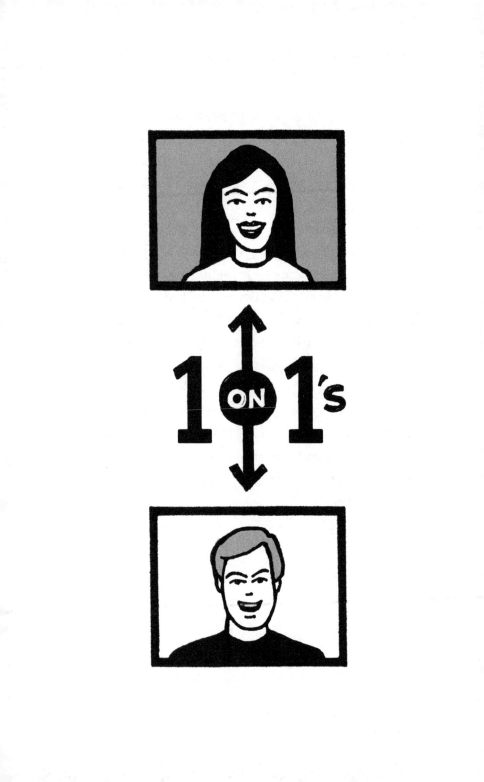

One-on-ones

While we advocate frequent check-ins with *all* your employees, it's a good idea to check in a bit more frequently with remote workers (since you'll bump into people in your office as a matter of course anyway). At 37signals, our schedule is a bit irregular, but we try to pick up the phone and talk with every remote person at least once every few months. In a perfect world we'd do it every month, but every few months has served us well.

We call these regular check-ins "one-on-ones," but other companies simply call them "check-ins" or "regulars." The key is to make them casual and conversational. This is a "what's up, how are things?" call more than a specific critique of a specific project or a response to a piece of work. These chats typically last twenty or thirty minutes, but it's good to keep an hour open—just in case. If the conversation is going well, you don't want to have to cut things short.

The goal here is really just to keep a consistent, open line of communication. These quick calls prevent issues and concerns from piling up without being addressed. Morale and motivation are fragile things, so you want to make sure to monitor the pulse of your remote workforce. Waiting six months or a year for the next formal review is too long.

Further, formal annual reviews are usually too big-picture to pick up on the small things. Formal reviews cover such things as long-range goals, salary adjustments, possible promotions, etc. But the *real* dangers are the small things—the concerns that creep up between annual check-ins.

The beauty of all this is that even though someone's a thousand miles away, everyone knows how to have a phone call. Just chat, nothing more, and see what comes up. You'll be surprised at how much you'll unearth during just your first one-on-one.

Remove the roadblocks

Getting stuff done while working remotely depends, first, on being able to make progress at all hours. It's no good twiddling your thumbs for three hours waiting for a manager to grant you permission, or hoping a coworker gets up soon so he or she can show you how something works in the remote world.

You don't really notice these roadblocks when you work 9am to 5pm in the same office as all your coworkers. Who cares if only Jeff is able to deploy a new version of the software if he's right across from you and all you have to do is ask? Or whether every refund has to be authorized by Jason before it goes out? The best way to ease the remote worker's plight is to do away with these roadblocks entirely. Start by empowering everyone to make decisions on their own. If the company is full of people whom nobody trusts to make decisions without layers of managerial review, then the company is full of the wrong people.

But really, that's rarely the case. What *is* the case is that people are often scared to make a decision because they work in an environment of retribution and blame. That style of work is very incompatible with remote work. As a manager, you have to accept the fact that people will make mistakes, but not intentionally, and that mistakes are the price of learning and self-sufficiency.

Second, you must make sure that people have access, by default, to everything they need. Most companies start out by adopting the reverse policy: everyone is only granted access to information and applications on a need-to-know basis. That's completely unnecessary. Unless you work in the military, or belong to one of the very rare firms that deal with super-confidential information—information that even trusted employees can't be trusted with—keeping these access barriers in place is just making it difficult for everyone to get their work done.

Part of the problem is the occasional pride that managers take in being Mr. or Ms. Roadblock. Having to be asked—even *courted*—gives them a certain perverse satisfaction. Do not discount how powerful this syndrome can be.

It's much better to recognize that certain people can take an interest in routing things through their desk even if it serves no logical purpose. Once you identify that tendency, you can work to replace the busywork of permissions and controls with the actual work of creating value for the business and its customers.

At 37signals we've created a number of ways to eradicate roadblocks. First, everyone gets a company credit card and is told to "spend wisely." There's no begging to spend money on needed equipment to get the work done, and there are no expense reports to fill out (just forward all receipts to an internal email address in case of an audit).

Second, workers at 37signals needn't ask permission to go on vacation or specify how much time they'll take. We tell them: just be reasonable, put it on the calendar, and coordinate with your coworkers. If you let them, humans have an amazing power to live up to your high expectations of reasonableness and responsibility.

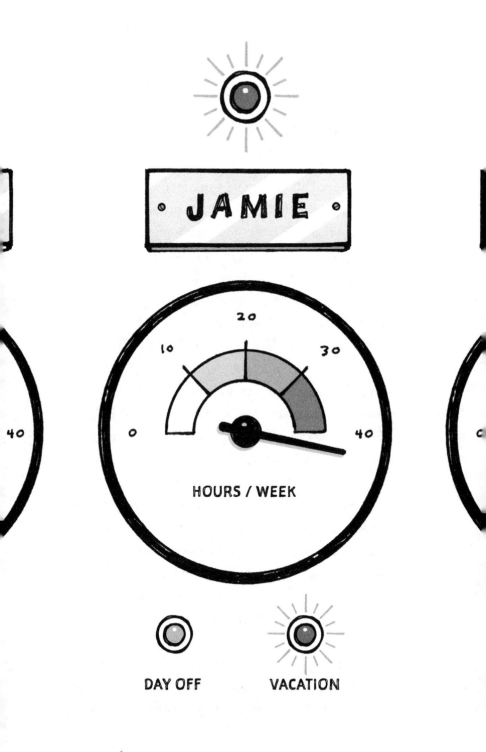

Be on the lookout for overwork, not underwork

If you've read about remote-work failures in the press, you might think that the major risk in setting your people free is that they'll turn into lazy, unproductive slackers. In reality, it's *over*work, not *under*work, that's the real enemy in a successful remote-working environment.

This is especially so when you have people working in multiple time zones and at all hours of the day. In the traditional office setup, people might stay a few hours after closing time, but they surely go home at some point. For remote workers, the lines are sometimes blurrier. If you have coworkers spread from Los Angeles to Moscow, you can be working almost around the clock, and there'll still be someone online to collaborate with.

But even when you and your colleagues are working together in the *same* time zone, it can be a problem. Working at home and living there means there's less delineation between the two parts of your life. You'll have all your files and all your equipment right at hand, so if you come up with an idea at 9pm, you can keep plowing through, even if you already put in more than adequate hours from 7am to 3pm.

The fact is, it's easy to turn work into your predominant hobby. *Hmmm, my partner is off to see friends for the evening? Might as well just finish up this one project. Ah, it's raining this Saturday? Well, I guess I could just finish that one report for the Tuesday conference call.*

This might sound like an employer's dream: workers putting in a ton of extra hours for no additional pay! But it's not. If work is all-consuming, the worker is far more likely to burn out. This is true even if the person loves what he does. Perhaps *especially* if he loves what he does, since it won't seem like a problem until it's too late.

It's everyone's job to be on the lookout for coworkers who are overworking themselves, but ultimately the responsibility lies with the managers and business owners to set the tone. It's much likelier to breed a culture of overwork if managers and owners are constantly putting in He-Man hours.

At 37signals, we fight this natural tendency toward overwork in a variety of ways. For example, from May to October, we give everyone an additional weekday off—more time to spend outside while the weather is nice and a good way to decompress from a hard-work winter. We also sponsor employees' hobbies and encourage people to take vacations by giving them tailored excursions of their choosing as holiday gifts.

In the same way that you don't want a gang of slackers, you also don't want a band of supermen. The best workers over the long term are people who put in sustainable hours. Not too much, not too little—just right. Forty hours a week on average usually does the trick.

Using scarcity to your advantage

When something's scarce, we tend to conserve, appreciate, respect, and value it. When something is abundant, we rarely think twice about how we use or spend it. Abundance and value are often opposites.

One obvious side effect of a remote workforce is reduced face time. On the surface that seems like a bad thing. Why make it harder for people to communicate? Why force people to phone, email, instant message, or video chat to have a conversation? Wouldn't communicating face-to-face be better?

Face-to-face conversations, and their first cousin, the meeting, can be great. When there's a complicated matter to discuss, one requiring a lot of interaction to sort through, few things beat a face-to-face meeting. However, when such meetings occur all the time, they begin to lose their value. Whereas before they'd been the perfect opportunity for a high-value exchange of information, they start to become routine, tired, played out, and, ultimately, an enormous waste of time. Questions that could have been answered in a few minutes via email or the phone turn into forty-five minute in-person conversations. Once in a while these gabfests are fine, but when they become the norm—when they're *abundant*—you've got a problem.

This is where remote working shines. When most conversations happen virtually—on the phone, via email, in Basecamp, over instant message, or in a Skype video chat—people actually look forward to these special opportunities for a face-to-face. The scarcity of such face time in remote working situations makes it seem that much more valuable. And as a result, something interesting happens: people don't waste the time. An awareness of scarcity makes them use it wisely.

We see this frequently at 37signals. Since most of us work remotely, we really value our occasional face time. A few times a year the whole company gets together for a week in Chicago. We hang out, talk a lot, get together in small groups. Over the course of these few days we're wildly productive. But if we did this constantly, we'd be wildly wasteful. It's the scarcity of the time together that makes it more valuable.

So go on—make face-to-face harder and less frequent and you'll see the value of these interactions go up, not down.

LIFE AS A
REMOTE WORKER

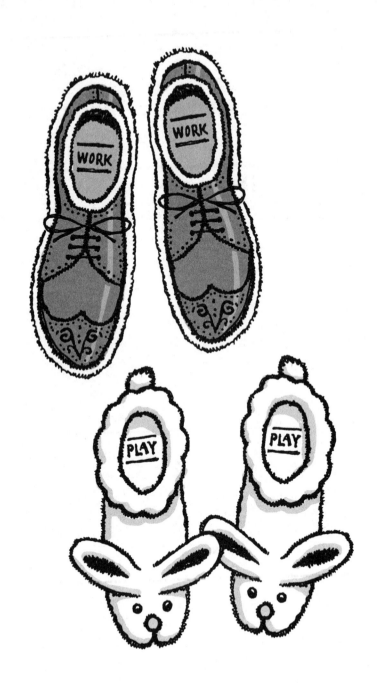

Building a routine

If nothing else, the standard 9am–5pm job with a commute at least has a solid routine going for it. The alarm goes off at roughly the same time every day, you head into the office on the train, you loosen the tie when you come back home, you pour yourself a scotch on the rocks . . . Okay, perhaps your routine isn't quite so 1950s, but you get the point.

Working from home offers you far greater freedom and flexibility. That might seem like an enviable dream to anyone stuck in a cubicle, counting down the minutes until the workday is officially over, but the reality is not quite so clear-cut. Without clear boundaries and routines, things can get murky.

If you don't have to be anywhere at a certain time, you can easily end up lying in bed until close to noon, just casually working away on the laptop. Or you can let work drift into that evening you're supposed to share with your spouse and kids. "Daaad, why aren't you watching the show with us?"

While some might be able to juggle that floating lifestyle, most people need some sort of routine—something they can stick to at least most of the time. We'll cover how to use different technologies for work and play in "Compute different," but, the fact is, there are many tricks you can employ to bring some structure to your day.

Take those comfy sweatpants, for example. They might be great for your physical comfort, but there's good reason to ponder whether they're a great fit for your state of mind. In the same way that there's a benefit to creating a separation between personal and work computing, it can also be helpful to separate the clothes you wear, depending whether you're in work or play mode.

This doesn't mean you have to dress up in a suit every day (but if that's what floats your boat, get that bow tie spinning!). We're merely suggesting that you demarcate the difference between work and play. Simply looking *presentable* is usually enough. One of our employees, Noah, likes to demarcate using his slippers: he has both a work set and a home set! Not everyone uses such props or even requires the mental separation they're meant to create, but if you're having trouble getting into work mode in the morning, try putting on some pants.

Another hack is to divide the day into chunks like Catch-up, Collaboration, and Serious Work. Some people prefer to use the mornings to catch up on email, industry news, and other low-intensity tasks, and then put their game face on for tearing through the tough stuff after lunch.

Depending on your time zone, you might do the

same but in reverse. For example, when David is working from Spain, his early mornings are great for getting stuff done before anyone from the United States is awake. After a mid-morning to afternoon break spent with his family, he uses the evenings for collaboration.

Finally, you can use the layout of your house as a switch. Make sure that real work only happens when you're in your dedicated home office. No checking work email or just getting a little more done in the living room or your bedroom.

Different strokes for different folks, so consider all these suggestions for how to build your personal routine as merely that—suggestions. If you're getting everything you need to get done just freewheeling, more power to you. But most people will need some semblance of structure to get the most out of working remotely. Find what works for you, pants or no pants!

Morning remote, afternoon local

As we've said elsewhere in this book, remote isn't all or nothing. Some people can be local, some can be remote. Or some days can be spent in the office, and some outside of the office.

But you can break it down even more. Days don't have to be all or nothing, either. You can slice the day in half and work remotely in the morning and at the office in the afternoon. In fact, that's a pretty popular pattern at 37signals.

Jason usually spends the mornings at home, then heads into the office around 11. That doesn't mean he starts work at 11. He starts around 7:30 or 8am. But he uses the morning to catch up on things that require zero office distractions, and then heads into the office for more collaborative work in the afternoon.

Flexibility is your friend here. Remote isn't binary. It's not here or there, this or that. In fact, for many, the hybrid approach is the right place to start. If you still want people in the office every day, change that requirement to every afternoon instead. Then let your troops have their mornings to themselves. You may be surprised to find out more work gets done this way.

Compute different

The gray line between work and play can be hard to see on the best of days, but almost impossible when you use the same computer for both. Sure, you could make sure to quit your programs for chat and email when you're off the clock, but you know you won't. That sort of discipline is not for mere mortals.

A more plausible, human strategy is to separate the two completely by using different devices: simply reserve one computer for work and another for fun.

This works doubly awesome if your fun device can't even *run* the programs needed to do your real work. Programming or designing might be technically possible on an iPad, but certainly not desirable.

You can back this up by confining the work computer to the home office. This works even better if you hook it up to enough keyboard, mouse, and monitor wires to make it a real hassle to disconnect. Having created conditions that necessitate getting off your comfy couch to check work email, your laziness will win most nights, leaving you to recharge your mental batteries until the morning.

We've found that using a completely different device—say, a tablet instead of a laptop—also brings a healthy change of scenery. If you sit in front of a keyboard all day long, it's great to "gear down" in the evening by using just taps and gestures. It makes computing feel like something other than work.

A similar effect is achieved by separating work and home accounts for email and chat. This is a bit harder to do, but the payoff is equally sweet. If your work email is available 24/7 on your tablet and phone, you probably won't be able to resist the temptation.

These days, having a second or third computing device in the house is so cheap that there's little excuse. Think of that iPad as your sweatpants—perfect for lounging around the house, but not something you'd think of taking to the office.

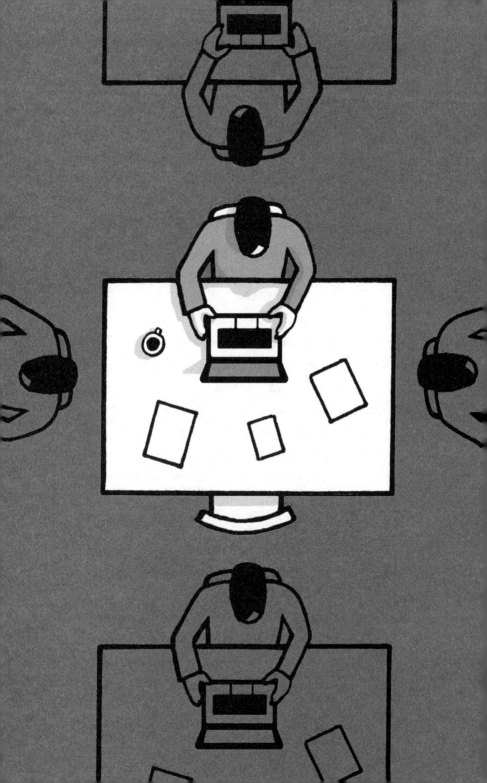

Working alone in a crowd

Getting away from the office is great for your productivity because nobody can disturb you in person. A boss or coworker might send you an email (which you can ignore for an hour) or they can try you on instant messenger (and find you "Away"), but they can't just barge in on your flow. They need your permission.

So what's not to like?

For some people, nothing. Certain remote workers will find, though, that it's actually harder to get into the flow when they're sitting in complete isolation. If that resonates, here's a simple strategy: Take your laptop and head to the nearest coffee shop with WiFi. There you'll get to work alone with no interruption from coworkers, but still enjoy the buzzing white noise of the crowd.

It sounds counterintuitive, but the presence of other people, even if you don't know them, can fool your mind into thinking that being productive is the only proper thing to do. Who really wants to be the slacker sitting in a coffee shop during working hours, watching silly cats on Reddit or playing a video game?

Of course, your hangout doesn't have to be a coffee shop. Try the library or a park or a co-working facility (which we'll soon discuss in detail in "No extra space at home").

And like remote work itself, the place you choose to go to when you want to take a break from home doesn't have to be an all-or-nothing proposition. For example, you can reserve driving downtown to the coffee shop for those occasions when you *really* need to ensure that not a second is spent on leisurely browsing.

Staying motivated

Motivation is the fuel of intellectual work. You can get several days' worth of work completed in one motivation-turboed afternoon. Or, when you're motivation starved, you can waste a week getting a day's worth of work done.

What exactly *is* the trick in a remote-working world? If you're a manager, how can you ensure that each member of your remote team is highly motivated? Should you threaten them with the stick or dangle the carrot?

As detailed by Alfie Kohn in his wonderful book *Punished by Rewards*:* neither. Trying to conjure motivation by means of rewards or threats is terribly ineffective. In fact, it's downright counterproductive.

Rather, the only reliable way to muster motivation is by encouraging people to work on the stuff they like and care about, *with* people they like and care about. There are no shortcuts.

At first, that's a hard nut to swallow. Especially for managers. "Work is not all fun and games" is a common objection. Perhaps. But why can't it be challenging, interesting, and engaging? Characterizing pleasure in work as "fun and games" belittles the intellectual stimulation of a job well done.

---

* http://www.alfiekohn.org/books/pbr.htm

So instead of trying to treat motivation as something that can be artificially ginned up with just the right tricks, treat it as a barometer of the quality of work and the work environment. If a worker's motivation is slumping, it's probably because the work is weakly defined or appears pointless, or because others on the team are acting like tools.

If you're working remotely and find yourself taking a week to do a day's work, that's a flashing red light and it should be heeded. The sooner you act on that message, the better.

But that's rarely how it goes. Most people suffering from a lack of motivation will blame themselves first. "Ah, it's because I'm such a procrastinator!" "Why can't I just get myself together?" The truth, more often than not, is that *you* are not the problem; it's the world you're working in.

If that's the case, the hard part is not just forcing yourself over the hump but having the courage to speak up and turn de-motivating work and environments into the opposite.

If you're a manager and notice that one of your employees is slacking, schedule a one-on-one and find out what's up. Is the person bored with a project that's not challenging enough, or are they feeling stuck and, in reaction, procrastinating to avoid a situation that feels impossible? See what you can do to get your employee back on track. The roadblock may be structural, or it may be more personal. Perhaps the employee is feeling burned out. That can be hard to discern when you're not working in the same office. Sometimes, just giving the person a couple weeks away from the job will be restorative enough to get him or her in the high-performing place they were previously.

At 37signals, we let employees who've worked with the company three years or more take a monthlong sabbatical if they feel like it. Sure, this won't work for every company, but if you have the slack and can handle it, it's a great way to give the employees who need a real break (not just a quick vacation) time away to focus on themselves, or their families, or whatever it is that might be keeping them from feeling fully motivated at work.

Motivation is pivotal to healthy lives and healthy companies. Make sure you're minding it.

Nomadic freedom

"When I retire, I'm going to travel the world" is a common dream, but why wait for retirement? If seeing the world is your passion, you shouldn't wait until old age to pursue it. And if you're working remotely, you can't use the "but I have a job" excuse to defer living.

We've had quite a few part- and full-time nomads employed at 37signals, and it's worked out great. As we've learned, once an employer accepts that an employee *can* function effectively while not working in a hub headquarters location such as Chicago or New York, the employee may as well be anywhere, tracing a route from Seville, to Amsterdam, to Malibu, to London—or anyplace else they're curious about.

Peter Baumgartner, founder of Lincoln Loop, moved with his wife and two children from Colorado to a beach town in Mexico, where he runs his web agency remotely (with employees in the United States, Canada, Europe, and New Zealand). He's thinking of spending the summer in Europe. No sabbatical needed!

Creative work that can be done remotely generally only requires a computer and an Internet connection. The computer you can bring with you, and nearly anywhere in the world you'll be hard-pressed not to find an Internet connection. Remember, the work doesn't care whether it's being done on a bench in Maui or a boat off the coast of Tampa (3G and LTE connections are plenty fine for most purposes).

That said, you still have to respect the laws of remote collaboration, such as overlapping with your teammates enough to ensure real-time communication (see "Thou shalt overlap"). But unless you travel to the other end of the world, that's immensely doable. In fact, if you're into exploring your new local habitat, you'll probably treasure the fact that work doesn't need to happen from 9am–5pm every day.

The nomadic lifestyle can be cheaper than you think too. If you don't burden yourself with a mortgage, car payment, cable TV, and other supposed necessities of modern living, there's usually more than enough left over for travel and accommodation.

Naturally, the nomadic life isn't for everyone. Or even for most, most of the time. But it's a choice available to remote workers that would have seemed ludicrous not too long ago: the luxury to see the world without being independently wealthy or giving up your career.

HOME

a CHANGE of Scenery

OFFICE

LIBRARY

CAFÉ

A change of scenery

One of the benefits of allowing your team to work remotely is that it gives them an opportunity to change their scenery as often as they like. We don't mean traveling to new and exotic places (though that's an option too, of course). We mean working from home some days, a coffee shop another day, a different coffee shop another day, the library another day, etc.

Routine has a tendency to numb your creativity. Waking up at the same time, taking the same transportation, traveling the same route, plopping down in the same chair at the same desk in the same office over and over and over isn't exactly a prescription for inspiration.

Changes of scenery, however, can lead to all sorts of new ideas. Mig, one of our designers at 37signals, uses his freedom to full advantage. Mig works in Chicago, but only comes into the office a few times a week, typically in the afternoon. His mornings are spent at different coffee shops around the city. The change of scenery, change of crowd, change of neighborhood, and change of menu helps him see similar things in new ways. He strongly believes that this variety translates to his work. More perspectives on the same problem is a good thing.

So don't think of working remotely as just shifting your routine from the office to the home. The choice of kitchen table versus cubicle is a false one. Instead, look at the remote option as an opportunity to be influenced by more things and to take in more perspectives than you normally might if you had to be in the same place at the same time every day.

Family time

The announcement by a troubled politician or CEO that he is stepping down to "spend more time with the family" is a cliché at this point, but that doesn't make the sentiment any less worthy. While nobody on their deathbed wishes they'd spent more time at the office, many sure do wish they'd spent more time with their family.

Once you factor in the hurried rush to get ready in the morning, the commute, and the lingering at the office after hours, the part of your day where you actually connect with your family seems frustratingly slim. Working remotely—especially from home and especially on flexible hours—can dramatically change that dynamic. Imagine eating breakfast with the family without the stress, taking half an hour over lunch to play in the yard together, or being there for a sick child without missing a whole day of work.

Having family close and available is a good way to counterbalance the loss of daily in-person contact with coworkers. And the corollary is that family people are more likely to be a good fit for remote working because of the existing social day-to-day interaction.

If, occasionally during your day, you're going to be interrupted by a tap on the shoulder, wouldn't you rather it be so you can give your partner a hand for a minute?

It's not exactly a stretch to see how everyone wins here. When the walk to the office is literally five seconds, family folks can put in the hours with less guilt and less stress. That means better work, better collaboration, and, in the end, better business results.

No extra space at home

Not everyone has a spare bedroom to turn into a home office, but that doesn't mean you can't work remotely. As we've discussed, working remotely doesn't have to mean working from home.

There is a wealth of options available to anyone looking for an office away from the office. The simplest, as we discuss in "Working alone in a crowd," is to use cafés. Plenty of people work full-time from an array of coffee shops.

But if you want something more permanent, you can also look into renting just a single desk from another company. For years we sublet four desks from Coudal Partners in Chicago. It was a cheap way to have a remote outpost away from our homes, with the added benefit of enjoying the fine people from Coudal. No reason that can't work for a single desk either.

There're also a growing number of co-working facilities popping up in major cities. They function on the same idea as subletting a single space or a few desks from another company, except *everyone* in the office is doing just that. It's a great way to achieve something halfway between a real office with coworkers and the stranger-in-a-crowd feeling of a coffee shop.

Regus, in 600 cities across 100 countries, has single

offices you can rent by the day, as well as "hot desks" you can share with other remote workers.* LiquidSpace is another example, with facilities in almost every U.S. state and plans to expand internationally. You can book online or use their app to specify when, where, and "how I work." You get to tell them the type of environment that best suits you, (whether that's a single office or a shared, open-air space)—and you also get to see photos of all the results before choosing.†

Finally, you can simply rent a plain-vanilla single suite in an office building somewhere. Regus provides those as well. While renting your own suite is likely to be the costliest option, it's probably a lot *less* costly than uprooting someone for another city.

---

* www.regus.com
† https://liquidspace.com

MAKING *Sure* YOU'RE NOT IGNORED

Making sure you're not ignored

One concern remote workers may have is that they will be ignored. "If I'm not seen, will I be heard?" "If I'm not hanging around, will people know who I am?" On the surface this is an understandable fear, but there's a very simple solution.

There are two fundamental ways *not* to be ignored at work. One is to make noise. The other is to make progress, to do exceptional work. Fortunately for remote workers, "the work" is the measure that matters.

When we hired our first full-time remote programmer back in 2005, we were blown away by the progress he made. He lived in Utah, nearly 1,400 miles away from our headquarters in Chicago. But he delivered incredible code in record time—all without working crazy hours. Even though we never saw his face, and rarely heard his voice, his work spoke loud and clear. He *produced*, so he couldn't be ignored.

Eight years later, Jamis, the programmer from Utah, is still with 37signals. Except that he finally left Utah. For Idaho.

CHAPTER

CONCLUSION

The quaint old office

*In thirty years' time, as technology moves forward
even further, people are going to look back
and wonder why offices ever existed.*

—RICHARD BRANSON, FOUNDER OF VIRGIN GROUP*

It's so hard to predict tipping points that most people find it easier to pretend they'll never happen. But a tipping point for remote work is coming. It may not be that the office completely ceases to exist, but its importance has peaked.

Life on the other side of the traditional office paradigm is simply too good for too many people. Progress on fundamental freedoms, like where to work, is largely cumulative. There might be setbacks here and there from poorly designed programs or misguided attempts at nostalgia, but they'll be mere blips in the long run.

Between now and the remote work–dominated future, the debate is likely to get more intense and the battle lines more sharply drawn. Remote work has already

---

* http://www.virgin.com/richard-branson/one-day-offices-will
-be-a-thing-of-the-past

progressed through the first two stages of Gandhi's model for change: "First they ignore you, then they laugh at you, then they fight you, then you win." We are squarely in the fighting stage—the toughest one—but it's also the last one before you win.

Michael Bloomberg, accomplished and respected mayor of New York, shows there's still work to be done in educating people about remote work's benefits, with this quote from the beginning of 2013:* "I've always said, telecommuting is one of the dumber ideas I've ever heard. Yes, there are some things you can do at home. But having a chat line is not the same thing as standing at the watercooler."

Old habits die hard. The more entrenched, the harder they die. To someone like Bloomberg, who over the course of decades has kept his coworkers close at hand (never more so than in his mayor's office, which with its warren of open cubicles mimics a trading floor), being able to peer out and "see" the work being done is as entrenched a habit as they come. Challenging such habits has always been a risky business. The world is flat right up until the day it's round.

---

* http://www.capitalnewyork.com/article/politics/2013/03/8071699/michael-bloomberg-agrees-marissa-mayer-telecommuting

Or as Harvey Dent from *Batman* said: "The night is darkest just before the dawn. And I promise you the dawn is coming."

Remote work is here, and it's here to stay. The only question is whether you'll be part of the early adopters, the early majority, the late majority, or the laggards.[*] The ship carrying the innovators has already sailed, but there are still plenty of vessels for the early adopters. Come on board.

---

[*] *Diffusion of Innovations,* Everett Rogers (1962)

THE REMOTE TOOLBOX

There have never been more tools to help make remote working possible. And they're so affordable too—many of them are priced with reasonable monthly subscription fees. Here's what's in our toolbox.

Basecamp. Basecamp is home base for all our projects. It's where we have group discussions, assign and track tasks, set up schedules on the calendar, brainstorm, share and discuss files, and make on-the-record decisions. No matter where you are, or where you work, Basecamp is available in your web browser or on your mobile phone (and it even works with plain old email!). On any given day we're running nearly thirty separate projects on Basecamp. Check out Basecamp at http://basecamp.com.

WebEx. WebEx is our go-to tool when we want to share a screen, give a product demo to someone who isn't in the office, and set up show-and-tell conference calls. Check out WebEx at http://webex.com. Great alternatives we sometimes use include Go-To-Meeting (http://gotomeeting.com) and Join.Me (http://join.me).

Know Your Company. If you're CEO or owner of a company with between twenty-five to seventy-five people, and you're having a hard time staying current on how your employees feel about your company, culture, leadership, management, workplace, decision making, etc., then Know Your Company is a godsend. It helps clue you in to all the unspoken realities of your company. This is especially important if your company is remote, since you see people less often and remote cultures are trickier to manage. Check out Know Your Company at http://knowyourcompany.com.

Skype. The old standby is still kicking for a reason— it's damn good! Excellent for international calling, conference calls, video conferences, and even basic screen sharing, it's hard to go wrong with Skype when you need to talk to people who aren't nearby. Extremely reliable, and widely adopted, and available for just about every platform under the sun. Check it out at http://skype.com.

Instant Messaging. For quick text-based chats with one other person, it's hard to beat Instant Messaging. If you're a Mac shop, iChat/Messages is a good option. If you're a Google shop, Gchat works real well. Or if you're technically inclined, you can set up a Jabber server (ask your IT guys).

Campfire. All day, every day, everyone in the company is logged into our Campfire group chat. Campfire creates a persistent chat room for your whole company. People can pop in and out and never feel left out of the conversation. It's a great place to ask a question when you just don't know who has the answer. You can even set up rooms for specific projects or teams inside your company. Check out Campfire at http://campfirenow.com.

Google Hangouts. The new kid on the block packs quite a punch. Google Hangouts is an incredibly easy way to fire up a private video conference with up to ten people. People can use their webcams on their laptops or cameras on their phones to jump in. The technology is top notch, and it has some great features that highlight the person talking so someone "has the floor." It really does a great job simulating being in a room together. We're using it more and more often for impromptu group video conferencing. Check it out at http://google.com/hangouts.

Dropbox. If you need to keep a trusted set of company files in one central place, and you want multiple people to have access to those files from their own computer—no matter where they live—Dropbox is a winner. Add a file to Dropbox and it'll be saved in the cloud and also on any computer, phone, or tablet you have where Dropbox is installed. It works across teams, across countries, across continents. It's like magic. Check it out at http://dropbox

.com. If you're a Microsoft shop, Skydrive may be a good option for you (http://skydrive.live.com).

Google Docs. If you need to collaborate on documents, spreadsheets, or PowerPoint-like presentations in real time, or if you just want to have a trusted spot for the latest version of a specific document, Google Docs is a great option. Check it out at http://docs.google.com.

Co-working spaces. One of the great remote-work movements in recent years has been the proliferation of "co-working spaces." These are places where people can rent a desk for a day, week, month, etc. It's perfect for remote workers who want to get out of the house a few days a week, or for those who need a desk while they're on the road. Regus (http://regus.com) has more locations around the world than anyone else, but there is also LiquidSpace (https://liquidspace.com) as well as local and regional co-working space directories, including Desktime (http://www.desktimeapp.com) and the Coworking Wiki (http://wiki.coworking.com/w/page/29303049/Directory).

ACKNOWLEDGMENTS

First, we'd like to thank all the employees of 37signals for their inspiration and for their review of the manuscript. They are living proof of how successful working remotely can be for both employees and employers.

In addition, we'd like to thank the following companies and individuals for letting us interview them about their remote work habits and experiences. Their feedback helped solidify many of the essays and inspired others.

Carabi + Co	Alex Carabi
Lincoln Loop	Peter Baumgartner
The Jellyvision Lab	Amanda Lannert
Accenture	Samuel Hyland and Jill Smart
Brightbox	John Leach
Herman Miller	Betty Hase
TextMaster	Benoit Laurent
Ideaware	Andrés Max
Fotolia	Oleg Tscheltzoff

FreeAgent	Olly Headey
BeBanjo	Jorge Gomez Sancha
HE:Labs	Pedro Marins
SimplySocial	Tyler Arnold
The IT Collective	Chris Hoffman
American Fidelity Assurance	Lindsay Sparks
SoftwareMill	Aleksandra Puchta
Perkins Coie	Craig Courter

Finally, we thank Jamie Heinemeier Hansson for all her help interviewing, researching, rewriting, and critiquing the manuscript. It would have been a far lesser book without her work.

To Jamie and Colt Heinemeier Hansson,
Working remotely has allowed the whole family to
spend more time together in more places.
Thank you both for your love and inspiration.
—DAVID HEINEMEIER HANSSON

For all those sitting in traffic right now.

—JASON FRIED

Published in the United States by Crown Business, an imprint of
the Crown Publishing Group, a division of Random House LLC, a
Penguin Random House Company, New York.
www.crownpublishing.com

CROWN BUSINESS is a trademark and CROWN and the Rising
Sun colophon are registered trademarks of Random House LLC.

Crown Business books are available at special discounts for bulk
purchases, for sales promotions, or corporate use. Special editions,
including personalized covers, excerpts of existing books, or books
with corporate logos, can be created in large quantities for special
needs. For more information, contact Premium Sales at
(212) 572-2232 or email specialmarkets@randomhouse.com.

Library of Congress Cataloging-in-Publication Data is available
upon request.

ISBN   978-0-8041-3750-8
eBook ISBN 978-0-8041-3751-5

PRINTED IN THE UNITED STATES OF AMERICA

Illustrations by Mike Rohde, rohdesign.com
Jacket design by Jamie Dihiansan, 37signals

10 9 8 7 6 5 4 3 2 1

FIRST EDITION

THANK YOU FOR READING OUR BOOK

We hope it inspires you to give remote working a shot. And if you're already working remotely, we hope it reassures you that you're ahead of the curve, not behind it.

Either way, we'd love to hear from you. If you have a story to share about making remote working work at your company, or if you're already a remote working champion, drop us a line at remote@37signals.com. We read every email, and respond to most—promise.

ABOUT 37SIGNALS

Our home page:
http://37signals.com

Our blog where we share a wide variety of ideas, stuff
we like, and our opinions:
http://37signals.com/svn

The official *Remote* book site:
http://37signals.com/remote

The official site for our other book, *Rework*:
http://37signals.com/rework

And, finally, if you want to know what we're up to,
subscribe to our we-won't-spam-you, irregularly
scheduled newsletter:
http://37signals.com/subscribe